A Guide to Early College and Dual Enrollment Programs

This is an accessible guide for school leaders and educators who seek to build, support, and expand effective early college and dual enrollment programs in their communities. One of the first books to bring together research in a practical way, this book is full of real stories, critical insights from leaders, teachers, and students, examples of what works and doesn't work, and strategies to help students successfully make an important jump in their lives, putting them on track to post-secondary education and a career. Whether you're starting a program from scratch or want to improve an existing dual enrollment and early college program, this book will provide you with the research base, tools, and resources to understand where you and your students fit into the national landscape, and provide guidance and inspiration on the journey to creating an effective program.

Russ Olwell is Associate Dean and Professor of Education at Merrimack College, USA. He has spent over a decade running youth mentoring and education programs.

Other Eye On Education Books Available from Routledge
(www.routledge.com/eyeoneducation)

Mentoring is a Verb: Strategies for Improving College and Career Readiness
Russ Olwell

The Strategy Playbook for Educational Leaders: Principles and Processes
Isobel Stevenson and Jennie Weiner

Unpacking Your learning Targets: Aligning Student Learning to Standards
Sean McWherter

Strategic Talent Leadership for Educators: A Practical Toolkit
Amy A. Holcombe

Becoming a Transformative Leader: A Guide to Creating Equitable Schools
Carolyn M. Shields

Bringing Innovative Practices to Your School: Lessons from International Schools
Jayson W. Richardson

Working with Students that Have Anxiety: Creative Connections and Practical Strategies
Beverley H. Johns, Donalyn Heise, Adrienne D. Hunter

Implicit Bias in Schools: A Practitioner's Guide
Gina Laura Gullo, Kelly Capatosto, and Cheryl Staats

Leadership in America's Best Urban Schools
Joseph F. Johnson, Jr, Cynthia L. Uline, and Lynne G. Perez

Leading Learning for ELL Students: Strategies for Success
Catherine Beck and Heidi Pace

A Guide to Early College and Dual Enrollment Programs

Designing and Implementing Programs for Student Achievement

Russ Olwell

Routledge
Taylor & Francis Group
NEW YORK AND LONDON

First published 2021
by Routledge
52 Vanderbilt Avenue, New York, NY 10017

and by Routledge
2 Park Square, Milton Park, Abingdon, Oxon, OX14 4RN

Routledge is an imprint of the Taylor & Francis Group, an informa business

© 2021 Taylor & Francis

The right of Russ Olwell to be identified as author of this work has been asserted by him in accordance with sections 77 and 78 of the Copyright, Designs and Patents Act 1988.

All rights reserved. No part of this book may be reprinted or reproduced or utilised in any form or by any electronic, mechanical, or other means, now known or hereafter invented, including photocopying and recording, or in any information storage or retrieval system, without permission in writing from the publishers.

Trademark notice: Product or corporate names may be trademarks or registered trademarks, and are used only for identification and explanation without intent to infringe.

Library of Congress Cataloging-in-Publication Data
A catalog record for this title has been requested

ISBN: 978-0-367-52851-5 (hbk)
ISBN: 978-0-367-53042-6 (pbk)
ISBN: 978-1-003-08025-1 (ebk)

Typeset in Optima
by Deanta Global Publishing Services, Chennai, India

To the talented students in the Lawrence Public School system, the dedicated staff and teachers that care for them every day, and the inspired leaders who have given them opportunities.

To MCW and to Lawrence Wright – your books are next!

Contents

Meet the Author ix
Preface x

SECTION ONE: CREATING POWERFUL PROGRAMS 1

1. Creating Powerful Early College and
   Dual Enrollment Programs 3

2. Creating Productive Relationships Between
   K-12 Schools and Higher Education Institutions 14

3. Leadership Challenges of Early College and Dual
   Enrollment Programs 27

SECTION TWO: SUPPORTING AND ENGAGING STUDENTS 39

4. Supporting Student Learning in Early College and Dual
   Enrollment Programs 41

5. Helping Early College and Dual Enrollment Students Map
   Their Future 60

6. Building Powerful STEM Experiences for Early College/
   Dual Enrollment Students 73

7. Opening Doors for Students: Social Sciences in the Early
   College/Dual Enrollment Programs 85

SECTION THREE: THE BROADER IMPACT OF EARLY COLLEGE AND DUAL ENROLLMENT PROGRAMS   97

8. How Early College and Dual Enrollment Programs Can Make a Difference for the Broader Community   99

9. Supporting Early College and Dual Enrollment Students' Health and Well-Being   109

10. Outside the Early College/Dual Enrollment Classroom: Extracurriculars, Sports, Clubs, and Work   117

SECTION FOUR: BUILDING SUSTAINABLE PROGRAMS   127

11. Measuring Impact to Build Sustainable Early College and Dual Enrollment Programs   129

Meet the Author

Russ Olwell is Professor of Education and Associate Dean in the School of Social Policy at Merrimack College in North Andover, Massachusetts. He was part of the team that developed the Merrimack College/Lawrence Public School early college program, which serves over 150 high school juniors and seniors every year. He has taught at the middle and high school level, and has worked with young people entering teaching for over 20 years. Olwell has written and presented extensively on topics such as youth mentorship, K-12 and college student development, and early college and dual enrollment development and impact.

Preface

You want to make a difference for the young people in your local schools and in your community, but a lot of what is being done in high schools does not seem to be working. Despite decades of effort, high school turnaround efforts remain difficult, and some efforts to close failing schools, transform existing schools, and build schools within a school have had more negative consequences than positive.

There are a lot of active and passionate programs in your community to serve youth, but without the academic component, many of their graduates struggle when they go away to college, and some show up back on the streets of your city with few credits and unpaid college bills, not to mention student loan debt.

As a result of your negative experiences, you look to efforts such as early college and dual enrollment, which, in the research literature, seem to be able to help a range of students (academically gifted, mid-range, at-risk) make significant academic strides. In addition, these programs seem to produce graduates who are confident and savvy about their transition to college, and who tend to graduate more quickly from two- and four-year degree programs.

While early college and dual enrollment programs do not offer a "silver bullet" or easy answer to the problems of America's high schools, they do point the way towards a system that has many fewer barriers between K-12 and higher education, and one that actively helps students make the successful leap from one system to another.

When I took a position at Merrimack College in Massachusetts in 2016, I had the opportunity to help create an early college program to serve students in the city of Lawrence. Before this, I had been involved tangentially at the Early College Alliance @ Eastern Michigan University, and knew about the power of the model. But I had spent most of my time working at EMU on programs such as GEAR UP and Upward Bound, which had a very different theory of change.

A GEAR UP program is a six-year effort to build the academic skills and confidence of students, to move them from the world of middle school to freshman year of college. Upward Bound similarly works with students for their high school experience to keep them on a path to university. It is hard for people outside the field to realize the sheer work that goes into these efforts, and the amazing commitment of staff to the students and families they work with.

A lot of us who work in early college and dual enrollment programs started our careers in these programs, and the shift to new models is striking. While TRIO and other college access programs go to great lengths to convince students they are ready for college, early college and dual enrollment programs lower the barriers to attend for students now, and allow students to discover for themselves that they are already capable of college level classes, provided they have the right level of support.

This shifts a considerable amount of work over to students – instantly they become part-time college students. To support them, faculty and staff need to provide just the right level of assistance – not too much to make the experience of college inauthentic, but enough to provide a greater chance of success.

The final results are striking, as will be detailed in this book. At the end of a number of early college or dual enrollment classes successfully taken, students feel far more confident and independent, and ready to tackle their next challenges. An early college or dual enrollment graduation ceremony is a celebration of what students have accomplished, and how families, faculty, and staff have served as vital supports. The students have accomplished something many would believe impossible, and we, the adults in the audience, feel lucky to serve as witnesses to their achievements.

This book is organized into four sections. The first, Creating Powerful Programs, is designed to help you launch a program, to rethink your present efforts, or to scale up a program to meet the needs of more students. Section two, Supporting and Engaging Students, details how to provide the student support that is critical to student success, and to engage these students academically across the curriculum. Section three discusses the broader impact of early college and dual enrollment programs, looking beyond the classroom to the student outside of class, on the sports field, and out into the community. Finally, the last section, Building Sustainable Programs, discusses the twin challenge of measuring the impact of your program, and using that data to build a sustainable funding stream.

Chapter Summaries

Section One: Creating Powerful Programs

Chapter 1: Creating Powerful Early College and Dual Enrollment Programs

This chapter details the key factors behind powerful early college and dual enrollment efforts, including leadership, connection to research, and high expectations for all students

Chapter 2: Creating Productive Relationships Between K-12 Schools and Higher Education Institutions

This chapter discusses the ways in which K-12 and higher education are able to find common ground in developing early college and dual enrollment programs, and the barriers that can emerge to creating a solid relationship.

Chapter 3: Leadership Challenges of Early College and Dual Enrollment Programs

This chapter discusses the challenges that school leaders face in developing early college and dual enrollment programs, including staffing, scheduling, and building common expectations across the K-12/higher education divide.

Section Two: Supporting and Engaging Students

Chapter 4: Supporting Student Learning in Early College and Dual Enrollment Programs

Student support is a critical factor in early college and dual enrollment efforts. This chapter details different ways of offering academic and other support, by both school/higher education personnel, and by those employed separately by the program.

Chapter 5: Helping Early College and Dual Enrollment Students Map Their Future

All students have a destination and goals beyond high school. This chapter details the ways in which early college and dual enrollment programs can help students navigate the worlds of college admissions, gap years, work, and the military.

Chapter 6: Building Powerful STEM Experiences for Early College/Dual Enrollment Students

STEM programs have long been a challenge for early college and dual enrollment programs. Drawing on research from successful programs, this chapter helps leaders navigate the best ways to deliver key skills and content in STEM to their students.

Chapter 7: Opening Doors for Students: Social Sciences in Early College/Dual Enrollment Programs

During high school, students are at an age when they can make huge intellectual gains, and are also able to understand that there is no right answer to many social and political questions. As a result, students can gain a great deal from social science classes at this age, and many can become interested in majoring in them in college.

Section Three: The Broader Impact of Early College and Dual Enrollment Programs

Chapter 8: How Early College and Dual Enrollment Programs Can Make a Difference for the Broader Community

The impact of programs goes far beyond the classroom walls. This chapter details the ways in which effective early college and dual enrollment programs can transform the community around them, bringing more two- and four-year graduates into the workforce and neighborhoods.

Chapter 9: Supporting Early College and Dual Enrollment Students' Health and Well-Being

Early college and dual enrollment students are people, as well as students. This chapter outlines some of the issues that young people face as a result of the stress of the programs they are enrolled in, and some ideas to help them thrive despite the pressure.

Chapter 10: Outside the Early College/Dual Enrollment Classroom: Extracurriculars, Sports, Clubs, and Work

While early college and dual enrollment students are busy with their coursework, the activities they do outside of school can add to the richness of their educational experience. This chapter describes some ways programs can help encourage students in many areas of their interest.

Section Four: Building Sustainable Programs

Chapter 11: Measuring Impact to Build Sustainable Early College and Dual Enrollment Programs

The toughest challenge of programs in many states is to obtain a sustainable funding stream to support their program. This chapter details strategies for collecting key data that can then be used to make the argument for public and/or private funding of programs.

Special Features

These short sections will help you get more out of this book as a guide for starting or scaling up an early college or dual enrollment program:

1. **Lead to Launch:** Indicated by an arrow, these are short pieces of advice from key leaders in the field about their experience creating and sustaining early college and dual enrollment programs.
2. **The Early College/Dual Enrollment Edge:** Indicated by a graphic of a plus sign, these short pieces summarize a key piece of research

on how early colleges can produce different results than traditional high schools.
3. **Real Students/Real Teachers**: Indicated by an outline of a person. These short segments profile a real early college/dual enrollment student, recent alumni, or teacher.
4. **Resource Toolbox:** Each chapter contains a succinct but impactful list of books, articles, and digital resources for further research and reading.

A Promise to the Reader...

This book will provide you with the research base, tools, and resources to get started, or to build on, your early college/dual enrollment journey. It will help you understand where you and your students fit into the national landscape, and provide some voices to help inspire you on the long and difficult journey to creating an effective program.

SECTION

One

Creating Powerful Programs

Creating Powerful Early College and Dual Enrollment Programs

The founding father of the accelerated college experience was, according to historian Ron Chernow (2004), Alexander Hamilton. Hamilton's intent to complete his degree and to save both time and money is at the core of today's early college and dual enrollment programs. (In this book, I will use the term "early college" programs for those that are 12 credits or more, take place on a college campus, and have a student support element. I use "dual enrollment" to describe programs that are fewer than 12 college credits and/or take place on a high school campus). In the world of education reform, early college and dual enrollment programs are "young, scrappy, and hungry" – only a few decades old, but still full of promise.

Early college and dual enrollment programs began decades ago as an experiment in gifted education. These programs were based on a radical premise – could high school students, if they were exposed to college coursework, rise to the occasion? Research in early college and dual enrollment programs demonstrates that, with the right design principles, high school students can achieve better results than college freshmen in college-level classes. These high school students, when they transition to full-time college enrollment, will achieve better outcomes as a result of these early college experiences. Additionally, students who are low-income, students of color, or whose family are immigrants are particularly helped by involvement in well-designed early colleges (Troutman et al., 2018; An, 2013).

However, while these programs can help students achieve higher GPAs, graduate on time, and save money, they are able to do so only if high schools and higher education collaborate to create a program that supports these students. Poorly implemented early college and dual enrollment programs can have a negative impact, giving students the false impression that they are ready for college, or can leave students with Fs in college classes that cause long-term harm. These Fs can follow students into college and affect their federal financial aid.

Alexander Hamilton, Early College Founding Father

If there is a figure who exemplifies the spirit of the early college, it is Alexander Hamilton, who as an immigrant and a believer in the acceleration of education, mirrors the strengths of many of our students and families in programs today. Hamilton, meeting with Princeton University's President Witherspoon, told him that he wanted to enter the college and advance with "as much rapidity as his exertions would enable him to do," graduating earlier than his peers. Witherspoon was impressed with Hamilton's preparation, but the trustees of Princeton were unwilling to go along with the proposal. In real life, unlike in the play, Hamilton took the news in stride and never punched the bursar as he does in Lin-Manuel Miranda's award-winning musical, *Hamilton*.

While Alexander Hamilton never attended an early college experience, he has many of the characteristics of students who are successful in early college efforts. Early college and dual enrollment efforts attract students who are seeking to complete the high school and college experiences more quickly and more affordably. They also tend to attract students from immigrant backgrounds, who are likely to favor academic pursuits over the social and athletic focus on many traditional high schools. They attract students and groups with something to prove, who view their academic achievement as defiance of how society seeks to define and pigeonhole them.

The Evolution of Early Colleges and Dual Enrollment

The early college and dual enrollment movements grew from efforts to allow students to begin the traditional college experience before age 18. Going to college "early" is a relative term. For students before the twentieth century in America, they might enroll at an age that was younger than a modern traditional American student might. Students would apply to enroll in college, and based on their academic achievements thus far, could be admitted when they proved they were ready to do so by way of classes taken or a test administered by the college itself.

What we think of now as "early college" grew out of efforts to allow students younger than traditional college age (i.e., 18–22) to do college level work. This grew out of the world of gifted education, where intellectual acceleration was the biggest part of the agenda for sending students to do college-level work at a pre-college age. In the late 1940s, proposals were introduced to reorganize all of education around this concept, with students taking classes in elementary school (grades K–6), then a middle/high school (grades 7–10), then a junior college (grades 10–14). The 1947 President's Commission for Higher Education for Democracy report suggested, "The time has come to provide financial assistance to competent students in the tenth through fourteenth grades who would not be able to continue [higher education] without such assistance." This radical change never gained traction.

Some of the earliest successful early college programs were residential, such as Simon's Rock, affiliated with Bard College, which began in 1966. The Simon's Rock effort to offer an early, but sheltered, college experience, dovetails with what we know about the cognitive development of young people (Simon's Rock College, History, 2019). By high school, many young people are able to tackle complex cognitive tasks required by a college curriculum. However, due to differential brain development, high school students lag in their decision-making and social skills, and therefore need support in these areas to be successful. Until 2000, efforts at early attendance at college remained a vibrant field, but a limited sized one, both in terms of enrollment and research. It was the intervention of a major foundation initiative that truly changed this field.

The Big Bang: How the Bill and Melinda Gates Foundation Changed Everything for Early College

While efforts to have students attend college early resonated with some educators, students, and families, the movement to send students to college early to provide intellectual challenge did not take off numerically. Before the year 2000, research and writing around early college centered on the needs of gifted students to do the level of college work that they were prepared to master. Some institutions, most notably Bard College, moved into the field of providing a broader early college experience, with its first New York City program opening in 2001, building off their experience with gifted education.

By the 2000s, a broader field of early college and dual enrollment was emerging, focused on using college credits earned in high school to encourage college attendance by urban and low-income students. Backed by the Bill and Melinda Gates Foundation beginning in 2002, this effort created networks of Early or Middle College high schools that provided the first test for the idea that providing students with college-level work while in high school would boost achievement at the time and provide for long-term educational positive outcomes. These efforts took root in some states (Texas and North Carolina), which provided the first large-scale evidence that these programs could have a positive impact. This provided both proof of concept, that early colleges could work, as well as proof that this model was scalable (Berger et al., 2013).

Non-profit organizations such as Jobs for the Future became a major player in the field as well, combining the Early College idea with Career and Technical Education, most often through community colleges. This might help students graduate from high school with credits towards an Associate's degree in a high demand field, sometimes with a corporate partner supporting these efforts (and hiring its graduates) (Jobs for the Future, 2019).

By 2010, much data had been collected on early colleges and dual enrollment, and these programs became known as an evidence-based strategy to boost high school achievement, as well as to increase the number of students attending and graduating from higher education. However, early colleges, once they ceased to be the focus of the Gates Foundation work, still struggle to interest either government or foundation investment, and require a good deal of local investment to get off the ground.

Lead to Launch: Bard College

Bard College has established early colleges across the country, and notes the following as key aspects that are needed to launch a successful new program:

- Strong local school leadership
- A real and documented need for early college in the community
- A school district willing to build a long-term financial model to support the effort
- A local philanthropic community committed to helping with startup costs

Bard College

Bard College, and its affiliated Simon's Rock Campus, has a unique role in the development of early college programs. Simon's Rock was created to give gifted students a chance to experience college-level work at an earlier age, while living in a supportive residential setting. In 1979, it was taken over by Bard College, which reshaped the early college model into a way to reach students in primarily urban high schools with an intellectual experience such as is typically provided to any outside highly elite private secondary schools.

Dr. Stephen Tremaine, Vice President at Bard College, notes that while early college is a movement that involves access and affordability for students, at its core, "it is largely about the idea that the intellectual life of high school students is richer than we think." Bard's work in New York City, which started in 2001, was designed to bring a residential small liberal arts college education to students in New York's public high schools. The motivation was to reach students who could do the work required at the college level, but were trapped in a high school system that was not meeting their needs: Tremaine says, "A lot of people in high school are being turned off rather than inspired to aim higher. The last years of high school are a poor use of time."

The goal of the early college was to provide an experience that would propel its students forward. "If early college is about giving young people the access to a full range of opportunities, and if you are a first-generation student, whatever exposure they get in high school is a stand in for the whole thing. If it looks malnourished, we risk turning you off to the whole endeavor." Bard went on to build on this work with a nationwide consortium of schools, all committed to improving and transforming public school systems. Tremaine offers, "We develop public schools in which high school and college work happen in one roof with one faculty – able to pay attention to and support the learning needs of adolescents in college curriculum – and build supports around their needs."

The goal of these schools is ambitious. Tremaine indicates, "Our premise is not to have to lower the bar or expectations. We are creating a higher bar for them. In an early college, the student body is fired up about this opportunity and step up to the challenge. This is not a student body you lower the bar for." Giving students only "access" to college is important, but "the extent to which the program serves access is only as good as commitment to quality." In spite of this track record of commitment, Bard has been limited in its expansion plans by funding, as public school districts do not always have the funding to support programs; philanthropic funds have been required to fill this gap.

What's in It for Higher Education?

While the benefits of early college high schools appear obvious to their proponents, the idea of having high schools on college campuses challenges many college and university educators. Professors worry about the different developmental needs of younger teenagers, and argue that they are not trained (or interested) in secondary education. They may fear being asked to water down their curriculum or adjust their grading practices to accommodate high schoolers. Concerns about privacy rights of minors and FERPA compliance often arise, as do issues of age-appropriate course content. Instructors and administrative staff alike balk at the idea of groups of teenagers causing disruptions on campus due to immaturity or "high-school" behavior. In some cases, dual enrollment or early college programs can be viewed as a threat to introductory class college enrollments (Gilbert, 2017), or as contributing to racial or income inequality (Miller et al., 2017).

The research on early college and dual enrollment programs strongly indicates that these programs are effective, and contribute to, rather than erode, the college's commitment to diversity, academic excellence, and equity. This research case has only become more compelling over the past decade, as researchers have moved from studying national data sets of students in early colleges to case studies of individual programs over time. Both types of studies have found that early college experiences can boost graduation rates, raise college GPAs, and shorten time to graduation among all students – including low income and minority students – when compared to their peers who did not attend early college programs (Troutman et al., 2018).

Case Study of Early College High School Success

Dr. Ellen Fischer, principal of Early College Alliance at Eastern Michigan University (EMU), analyzed the outcomes of her program, and was able to compare EMU's early college students directly to the students they are sitting in class with – traditional college first-year students. When examined head to head, some key results stand out: Early college graduates have earned Bachelor's Degrees at far higher rates than their non-ECA peers, with most ECA graduates continuing their education at EMU. Early college students were equal or greater in diversity than their peers across the county, and African-American students benefited greatly from early college enrollment and were able to graduate at a higher rate as a result. The impact for African-American students stood out, as they were far more successful in the early college program than in other school systems in the county and throughout the state, both urban and suburban, low-income and high-income.

Higher education leaders can learn lessons from the early college and dual enrollment experiences, and can apply what works with early college students to traditional first-year students. Early college programs have developed facilitated support for students as they move into college classes, and have developed expertise in the type of teaching, mentoring, and advising that allows students to thrive. College leaders can emulate the focus that early colleges have on social/emotional learning. Early college students learn non-academic keys to successfully navigating a college classroom, and learn explicitly how to interact with professors, how to seek help when not succeeding in class, and how to learn from failure. In addition, they directly learn what college-readiness researcher David Conley (2007) terms "key academic behaviors," such as note-taking and study skills. Finally, early colleges can provide a pipeline of students who are ready to be successful on campus, and who are used to navigating the foibles of that system. While university marketing can spend up to $5,000 per enrolled student to recruit, early college students are already in the classroom and the hall, and usually just need to be reminded to apply on time.

What K-12 Schools Get Out of Early Colleges

K-12 school systems can use early colleges to meet a number of challenges. First, early colleges provide an authentic level of high expectations for students to meet. It is impossible to overstate the importance of high expectations – with support to help them meet those expectations – for high school students, particularly for those in families with little (or negative) college experience. Early colleges demonstrate to students what is needed in a college course or majors by having them take a class in the subject on a real campus with a real professor – the difference between "showing" and "telling." In many ways, early colleges simply lift the barriers between students and the college experience and give them a chance to succeed, a powerful act of trust.

K-12 systems can also use early colleges to manage costs while expanding programs. Moving advanced courses to a college or community college campus keeps the school system from having to recruit teachers in narrow subjects, staffing for a small number of students interested in highly advanced coursework. What is learned from the early college experience can help K-12 districts rethink their high school and middle school offerings, giving them a real-time sense of what has worked and not worked at the district level. Early colleges also draw students and families back into the district who left because of low academic performance, often to private schools. Finally, early college programs, designed well, boost diversity and the range of students served.

For parents and students, right now, cost is the major driver that shapes interest in early college. The costs of higher education, and the lack of ways to pay for it, have increased the demand for and interest in early college programs, to the point where other motivations (interesting coursework, getting ahead in studies, increased skills) have taken a back seat. Particularly for first-generation students, or those from immigrant backgrounds, the need to minimize college costs, loan debt, and to embark on a career, are all at the top of the agenda, with other motivations coming into focus if the first criteria are met. College and dual enrollment programs can prove to first-generation college students, and to their families, that they can be successful in college, fighting back the voices in their head, their family, and their community, that might express doubt about the process.

For communities, early college and dual enrollments programs offer a unique resource that can be used to boost the overall economy of the region. Early colleges are attractive to recruit people to live in an area, and they are a great way to spotlight educational achievement. In the long term, by enabling more people in the community to achieve a college degree, they can help build a sustainable economic base for a city or a region.

Early College/Dual Enrollment Edge:

Dr. Jack Leonard's research demonstrates that to start and thrive, early college and dual enrollment programs need:

- Entrepreneurial leaders willing to take risks and bend some rules
- Commitment from both the higher education and K-12 side
- Work to engage with all relevant nuts and bolts of partnership
- Leaders who succeed the founders, who are equally committed to the effort

Early College and Dual Enrollment: What's in It for Whom?

Most of us involved in higher education feel our eyes start to glaze over when someone asks, "What is in it for us in early college?" Rather than reacting defensively to the question, education researcher Jack Leonard (2013), turned this into a research question, identifying the seven different ways in which early college and dual enrollment stakeholders think about the effort. As Leonard described these theories and applied them to early college/dual enrollment:

1. Efficiency: Early college programs allow colleges and school districts to access a resource at a lower cost than to develop those resources themselves, such as college classes. An early college or dual enrollment program is a way of efficiently buying college credits on behalf of families, who otherwise would be paying a far higher sticker price.

2. Resource dependence: Institutions are not able to do everything for themselves, and enter into partnerships to gain access to resources they may not be able to develop. High schools would need to invest in professional development to create instructors ready to teach college-level classes. It may be easier to develop an early college program to access this resource external to the K-12 school.

3. Leverage: Colleges or high schools can pursue early college or dual enrollment to grow in their marketing efforts or in prestige, or to tap new sources of revenue. Some college dual enrollment programs have developed a statewide constituency (University of Connecticut), and some early college programs have spread to multiple sites (Bard).

4. Learning: Institutions can come together to learn more about their own operations as well as their partners' operations. Alas, educational institutions are no more likely than any other institution to pursue learning.

5. Legitimacy: Institutions may enter into early college or dual enrollment efforts because the public, and their stakeholders, expect them to as part of their commitment to the common good.

6. Stakeholders: The relationships of individual and groups of people may be key to early college and dual enrollment efforts. Examples might include personal friendship between a superintendent and a college president that serves as a catalyst.

7. Domain focus: Stakeholders may come together in early college/dual enrollment efforts to help address a major national problem, such as lack of college readiness, with the proposed program pointing the way to a solution.

Resource Toolbox

An, B.P. (2013). The Impact of Dual Enrollment on College Degree Attainment. *Educational Evaluation and Policy Analysis, 35*(1), 57–75.

Berger, A., Turk-Bicakci, L., Garet, M., Song, M., Knudson, J., Haxton, C., ... & Keating, K. (2013). Early College, Early Success: Early College High School Initiative Impact Study. *American Institutes for Research.*

Chernow, R. (2004). *Alexander Hamilton.* New York: Penguin Books.

Conley, D. (2007). Redefining College Readiness. http://www.aypf.org/documents/RedefiningCollegeReadiness.pdf. Retrieved November 14, 2020.

Fischer, E.L. (2016). Laying the Foundation: An Investigation of Bachelor's Degree Attainment Rates of Early College High School Graduates. Master's Theses and Doctoral Dissertations. Paper 668. Eastern Michigan University. https://commons.emich.edu/theses/668. Retrieved November 14, 2020.

Gilbert, E. (2017). How Dual Enrollment Contributes to Inequality. *Chronicle of Higher Education*, November 5. https://www.chronicle.com/article/how-dual-enrollment-contributes-to-inequality/. Retrieved November 14, 2020.

Leonard, J. (2013). Negotiated Issues in an Early College Partnership: Description and Understanding through Interorganizational Theory. *Current Issues in Education, 16*(3).

Miller, T., Kosiewicz, H., Wang, E.L., Marwah, E., Delhommer, S. and Daugherty, L. (2017). *Dual Credit Education in Texas: Interim Report.* RAND Corporation: Santa Monica, CA. https://www.rand.org/pubs/research_reports/RR2043.html. Retrieved November 14, 2020.

Troutman, D., Hendrix-Soto, A., Creusere, M. and Mayer, E. (2018). *Dual Credit and Success in College.* University of Texas System. Austin, Texas.

United States. President's Commission on Higher Education., Zook, G.F. (1947). *Higher Education for American Democracy: A Report.* Washington, DC: U. S. Govt. Print. Off.

Vargas, J. (2019). Breaking the Boundaries between High School and College: How to Scale Success for Low-Income Students. Jobs for the Future. https://www.jff.org/resources/breaking-boundaries-between-high-school-and-college-how-scale-success-low-income-students/. Retrieved November 14, 2020.

Creating Productive Relationships Between K-12 Schools and Higher Education Institutions

Early college and dual enrollment programs are, by their nature, hybrid institutions, a mix of the higher education and K-12 systems. Rather than become either college programs for younger students, or 13th and 14th grade of high school, good early college and dual enrollment programs build on the institutions that birthed them, and then develop further on their own. Unfortunately, not many leaders in the education system really have experience of both sides of the K-12/higher education divide. This can lead to mistrust, misunderstandings, and the belief that the other institution has much more money and resources than it is letting on. Most higher education administrators have spent all of their adult lives in colleges and universities, and are used to the spoken and unspoken rules that govern this world. Most leaders in the K-12 arena have spent their lives working with students and teachers, mostly in a highly transparent public sector, governed by law and policy.

It often takes a full planning year for these K-12 and higher education institutions to see one another's perspective, and from there, it often takes having students in common for the two groups to begin to develop a perspective outside their institutional home. As staff and faculty see a cohort of students move through the program, graduate, and move on to college, they become more invested in shared success than in their own home institution's position.

The Importance of College and K-12 Leadership for Early College and Dual Enrollment Programs

When it comes to early college and dual enrollment, if the leadership of the organizations does not truly embrace these programs, and move their own institution to address the needs of the program, the program will eventually shrivel and die. At a college, any number of offices, if they refuse cooperation, can sink a program with a single decision against it. The legal office can decide that it is too risky for lawsuits; the provost's office can decide that it endangers accreditation; the business office can decide it is too costly; the registrar can refuse to assign rooms. Within the K-12 systems, the superintendent and principals can switch priorities at the close of a school year, leaving the program without the staff and funding they need.

I have never seen a truly excellent early college or dual enrollment effort launched without a leadership that is willing to say "make it happen" and sometimes "make it work." In some cases, this leadership is more enthusiastic than in others. But early college and dual enrollment programs, unlike many educational innovations, require visionary leadership at the top, and cannot entirely rely on grassroots efforts of teachers or parents. There are just too many important moving parts, and too many decisions that need to be made to move them forward.

This enthusiastic and visionary person at the top is critical, but so are the levels of organization beneath this. The administration beneath the top level creates the program's infrastructure, solves problems as they come along, and generally keeps the program together. As someone familiar with programs across the state said "at every successful program, I can point to both a top leadership and to the next level who really do the work, and to people who it is in their job description to get the programs to work." Without all these levels, a single schedule change can bring a program to a halt.

The most important part of leadership in developing early college and dual enrollment programs is vision – being able to picture in your mind's eye the way the program should run, and then taking steps to get there. Often, leaders bring the model with them when they switch institutions, and having seen it work wonders in one set of circumstances, are able to adapt it to new places. But folks who do not really get the model, or view it as just colleges offering a discount, are not often going to change their views. There is a level of vision and belief that is vital for starting an early college or dual enrollment program, and must be shared across the whole team.

Lead to Launch: Pres. Chrisopher Hopey, Merrimack College

President Hopey, before founding the early college program at Merrimack College, helped create Foundation Year at Northeastern University, providing a path to college for Boston Public School students. His advice for leaders founding a new program includes:

1. Creating effective programs takes both strong leadership and strong faculty and staff to work with the students. The faculty needs to be as talented as any on campus, but focused on teaching students, not on research and publishing.
2. Programs need to build skills in key academic areas, such as literacy, as well as provide socialization on the campus. Programs that bring students to a campus, and introduce them to college faculty, are needed to help high school students become truly ready for what comes next.
3. In the future, dual enrollment and early college programs will become more widespread as a way of higher education reaching high school juniors and seniors, acquiring enough credits to cut a year of tuition off their time to degree.

Creating Connections through Dual Enrollment

Dual enrollment programs have a long history, dating back to 1955, but have been flying below the radar for much of that time. The first program to take root, the University of Connecticut Dual Enrollment Program, was germinated in the experience of World War II, when colleges and universities nationwide saw their primary audience (young men) diverted into national service. This raised the issue of whether at least some high school students, such as academically talented juniors and seniors, might fill this gap in enrollment on campus.

At the University of Connecticut, Provost Albert Waugh was grappling with the same issues plaguing every administrator who wanted to devise early college experiences – he proposed a program to give talented high school students a chance to experience collegiate level work, but his infrastructure of buildings and instructors was not sufficient to address the needs of the students already in the pipeline for enrollment. As a result, Waugh and Connecticut devised the first "dual enrollment" option, with high school students taking college-level work at their high school building, presided over by a high school staff member approved for this work. The initial slate of schools was just a handful, but over time the network has expanded to include a wider range of districts, with an intentional focus on urban districts.

Dual enrollment's emergence in the 1940s and 1950s reflects several key issues of the period. The first was the ebbs and flows of the supply of college students during the period – down to a trickle during World War II, then rising with the GI Bill, but with infrastructure and policy always catching up to demographic change. The dual enrollment effort also fits with the criticism of high schools during the 1950s, particularly the charge leveled by Harvard President James Conant that high schools were not addressing the needs of the most talented of their students, particularly in areas such as math and science. While not designed to meet this cold war/Sputnik challenge in STEM education, dual enrollment could be viewed as a simple solution to it (Grant 2019).

Real Student: Brian Boecherer

- Dual enrollment student in high school.
- Inspired to work harder by a C on a paper in a dual enrollment class.
- Worked through college and graduate school for dual enrollment program.
- Now directs University of Connecticut dual enrollment program.

What Makes Dual Enrollment Programs Powerful?

Brian Boecherer, director of the University of Connecticut program, was himself a student in the program in high school. What he remembers most about his experience in high school was the first time he got a C on a paper in a dual enrollment class. The faculty member encouraged him to work more on his writing, and Boecherer did, earning stronger grades as he went along. This experience of being academically challenged, and rising to the challenge, is a key ingredient in dual enrollment coursework. Boecherer says that the students who do well in the program are those that have grit, and the program itself aims to build that grit, so that students, even when facing academic frustration, feel supported by faculty to push forward, improving their academic work and their grades.

The key ingredient to the process is selection and professional development of faculty. According to Boecherer, if high school teachers are asking "what's in it for me?" they are the wrong choice. In order to qualify as dual enrollment teachers, candidates need to submit evidence of their background and qualifications, reviewed by the college. Some candidates may need to take further coursework to qualify, and according to Boecherer, the strongest dual enrollment teachers are the ones who embrace this process. Professional development, as well as greater connection to UConn's academic departments follow, and those teachers who persist in the program get a great deal out of it.

Boecherer is proud of the way in which his dual enrollment program has grown from being a program that served some of the state to one that reaches many more high schools. The program has built agreements with all of the urban school districts in the state, and is also mindful of the needs of rural schools, which often lack the resources to offer many high-level classes. The program has diversified its curriculum, now offering 75 classes per year, which allows a broader range of students to explore their gifts, whether standard offerings such as Calculus and Chemistry, or fields such as Spanish, Environmental Science, or Agricultural Science.

Work with urban schools has involved a lot of outreach and visiting. The key to signing on urban schools to the program has been in person on site visits, with the program director making sure that they stop by urban high schools whenever in the city in question. This constant contact and offer of help has earned the program many schools that otherwise would have ignored dual enrollment as an option, and brought many more urban teachers and students into the program as a result. Designating resources for fee waivers for students receiving free or reduced lunch or schools in which 80%+ of students receive free/reduced lunch has also allowed the full range of students in the state to access the program.

Memoranda of Understanding and Policy Documents

Memoranda of understanding (MOUs) are legal documents that lay out the institutions involved in a program, the responsibilities of both sides, how decisions are made, and how the relationship can be terminated. This might sound like a prenuptial agreement for a marriage, but MOUs are fundamentally a way for friends who go into an enterprise together to remain friends, as it provides a framework for a relationship that exists on paper, not in the minds of the parties involved.

Strong and sustainable programs need a few key elements in an MOU to really keep them alive over the long term. A memorandum of understanding that lays out clearly, without ideals, what each side will get and give to this effort. At the end of the day, most early college and dual enrollment programs are the purchase of college credits, often at a discount. Colleges are providing instruction and assessment to high school students. Personnel involved in the program need to be paid, and expenses that are incurred need to have someone who will step up and take responsibility for them. MOUs are a legal way of capturing these key relationships and assigning important roles to the institutions involved.

MOUs:

- Lay out the mission of each instruction involved, and how this new initiative fits into both the existing missions and the new mission of the program.
- Provide a calendar for regular review and resigning (usually once per year), and ask partners to recommit to efforts rather than just let them passively linger.
- Define the status of students – in which ways they are treated as college students and in which ways as high school students. This includes

> access to areas such as the library, fitness center, tutoring services, and athletic events.
> Define key policies for each side of the relationship, and can include areas such as scheduling, qualifications, admissions, and budget.

My wise colleague Dr. Christine Shaw told me to separate out policy aspects of the early college from the legal issues of the MOU. The policy document allows a steering committee to make decisions without going back and revising an MOU that would require re-review by the legal office and sign off by two busy CEOs. Likewise, many MOUs refer to budget information but place an official budget for each year as an appendix. When disputes arise in the day-to-day operations of an early college or a dual enrollment program, going back to the MOU is a key step in resolving disputes. In a context in which both higher education and K-12 organizations experience leadership turnover, foundational documents help everyone around the table grasp what was agreed to in the past.

Connecting the Organizations

The two CEOs of the school system and college should meet at least once per year to update each other on the program and where it stands. This does not have to be a long meeting, but is symbolically and practically important for the program. Particularly as there are leadership transitions and shifts of priorities, it is vital that the heads of both organizations continue to buy into and actively support early college and dual enrollment efforts. Both sides also need to talk about how early college and dual enrollment strategies fit into overall institutional strategic planning and efforts, so that they are not left behind as conditions shift. This can be a 35,000-foot discussion, but it needs to take place, to counter the danger that these programs can become disconnected from the overall institutional mission, ending in neglect, or in programs going rogue.

Steering Committees

Dual enrollment and early college programs do not fit well within the committee structures of high school or higher education. K-12 committees can often do a good job gathering information across teachers, administrators, students, and parents, but are hard to extend to outside stakeholders. Traditional higher education committees are good at managing the status quo, and have a hard time with any innovative structures.

Steering committees for early college and dual enrollment programs often draw from principals, deans, department heads, and student support areas. Key areas such as the registrar's office and admissions are also important to have at the table. After an initial launch period, faculty teaching early college classes are not ideal for the committee, as the group may be hearing about school and student feedback about courses that can be tough to hear. Instead, the group needs to contain the minimum number of decision makers needed to address the problems that the program will run into during the year.

Over time, these committees start to reflect less the sum of individual roles and interests, and begin to focus on problem-solving for a shared group of students. Once people around the table begin to see the students as a joint responsibility, the group begins to bridge the K-12/higher education divide, and to really focus on program effectiveness and student success.

These committees should also be able to move out of the weeds of everyday running of the program to larger policy issues.

Student Support

Smaller committees can take on issues such as individual student needs, or problems seen in classes. Rather than thinking of student support as being remedial and reactive (a student is failing biology, what can we do?) student support can be built into the early college/dual enrollment program from the start. As we learn more about which classes require the most support, help such as undergraduate teaching assistants, writing fellows, and peer support can be built into the class.

Regardless of the proactive services implemented, program staff will need to help contact and access support for students in the program who are experiencing in or out of class difficulties. In our three years of operation, our early college has endured a massive gas explosion, a threatened school shooting, and a global pandemic, all requiring a coordinated program response to support students. In addition, students have struggled with mental health issues, foster care placement, long distance transportation needs, and other barriers.

Over time, college faculty and staff become more accustomed to and empathetic about the needs of K-12 students, and gain more respect for the barriers encountered everyday by K-12 teachers and staff. They often also learn more about the range of issues that can interfere with learning for K-12 students, and can rethink their own approach to issues such as extensions for papers and tests that are due to factors outside of student control.

Budget and Costs

Making a budget can be a painful and sobering experience for early colleges and dual enrollment programs. Without dedicated support at the state or local level, early college and dual enrollment programs are often stuck cobbling together a budget from the separate and already-stretched K-12 and higher education budgets. However grim the task may seem it is important for partners to develop and agree on a joint budget for the program at least once per year.

The key items for these budgets include personnel (on both sides), tuition costs, transportation, books, software, laboratory, and safety supplies. In kind contributions, such as administrator time, should be included as well. Some of these costs will be fixed (most personnel costs) and some are frustratingly variable (books and software that faculty assign for their course). This process will be educational for both sides, as often college administrators have no idea the extra costs imposed on students by idiosyncratic faculty choice – information that may feed back into the higher education system for further examination.

Taking an honest look at the budget can help identify where there are systemic problems in the way business is done in either institution. In the case of higher education, involvement in early college and dual enrollment can show, in black and white, how books and software expenses, added by faculty members, can become more of a burden on the program than personnel expenses for the program. Involvement in these efforts has convinced many in higher education about the importance of open educational resources for courses, which reduce the expense using free online materials rather than a textbook.

Early college and dual enrollment programs are not designed to be primarily a cost saving. While institutions may view early college or dual enrollment as a way to avoid hiring more teachers to teach college-level classes, or as a way to put students in the seats of under-enrolled college classes, good programs require more resources for student support. As Massachusetts Commissioner of Higher Education Carlos Santiago said, "Early college means you invest more, not that you spend less." While teachers' unions in both the K-12 and the higher education systems have worried about erosion of jobs in early college or dual enrollment programs, if the program involves full support of the students in the high school, this job erosion does not take place.

The Importance of Special Events and Milestones

There are not many moments when K-12 and higher education institutions share responsibility for the same students at the same time. Usually, the two systems deal with students in series, with K-12 teachers and administrators handing off the students to us when they enroll in college and arrive on campus. Many times, the relationship between K-12 and higher education shows this rift – K-12 teachers complain that their students, even top students, are less successful than they should be in college; college faculty complains that students are not prepared by the K-12 system to do their work in the college classroom.

This is why it is vital to create events for early college and dual enrollment programs that span this gap, and bring people together in a common celebration of students' achievement and potential. Graduations are a key moment when people can gather and celebrate the students' individual and collective achievements. At Merrimack College, to celebrate the graduation of our early college students, we held a ceremony for them and their families in our campus church. The ceremony included addresses by two student speakers, a speech by one of our professors, and a bilingual song played on guitar by another professor. Students and families lingered into the night after the ceremony was over, taking pictures all over the church.

I have been to many graduations, both high school and college, but this one was unique. The people on stage – the high school principal and assistant principal, the head of the early college program, administrators from the college, were all up on the same stage, distributing certificates and tassels. Every other ceremony or event I have seen is the property of one group or the other, with one staff presenting honors and the other consigned to the audience. This evening, complete with Spanish translation for families, showed how early college programs can transform the relationship between K-12 and higher education.

These kinds of events, launching or closing an academic year, help honor the work of students, faculty, and staff, but also to rally support for early college programs, and make visible the hard work that is being done. Much of the magic of early college takes place behind the scenes – students studying, teachers connecting to students, registrars processing grades. It is only at events such as an orientation or graduation that early college and dual enrollment programs get the visibility they deserve.

The Early College/Dual Enrollment Edge:
Dual enrollment programs in Massachusetts have demonstrated:
- Mid-range students can benefit from dual enrollment classes.
- Students need academic support to benefit from these offerings.
- Paying some part of the cost can build buy in and commitment from families.

Dual Enrollment and the Middle Student

Dr. Jack Leonard came to the field of dual enrollment and early college as a result of his experience as a high school teacher and principal, and taking a position teaching at the University of Massachusetts at Boston. He served as the evaluator for a project in Amesbury, Massachusetts that sought to develop a dual enrollment/early college program for students in the middle of the achievement range. This program sought to reach a different population than was traditionally highly engaged at the high school – top achieving students taking all Advanced Placement classes. Leonard came to early college through visiting sites in New York City, where he got to see examples of programs where students who otherwise would not be headed for college were being involved in programs, and were highly successful.

As an administrator, Leonard had worked in Boston to try to get more opportunities for his students to take classes at a local community college, but found many barriers to the type of program he wanted. Tests such as the Accuplacer were used to screen students, and as a result, many students who might benefit from the program were excluded from the start. Leonard found that to develop strong programs, higher education partners needed to be much more flexible than they traditionally had been, and needed to be willing to bend some of their rules to implement a program at scale.

Leonard researched how colleges and high schools negotiate agreements to create programs, and found that there were issues that did not emerge in early discussion, but could derail efforts to create strong early college programs. For instance, if administrators did not agree on issues involving union contracts at the college or K-12 level, the teacher/professor evaluation process, and potential financial aid issues, the whole project could be derailed.

While counter to much of the equity thrust of early college literature, Leonard concluded in his research that some charge for college credit to students and families was a positive motivator. Without the revenue from these charges, programs had no way to pay out any of the extra expenses. More importantly, even a token charge gave students and families much more investment in the program, and discouraged students from signing up and immediately withdrawing from the program when the work became challenging. He found that the vast majority of families dreamed of their children going to college, and did not mind paying a discounted fee for the credit received while in high school.

Leonard views early college as a case study of an innovation that requires strong entrepreneurial leadership to launch on both sides – higher education and K-12. However, he saw that for the programs he worked with, the next leaders after the founders moved on or retired were also critical, and if they did not buy into early college, it could wither quickly. He also views early college as a reform that does not need to "scale up," but can be developed to meet local needs and adapted to meet the needs of many different districts, urban, suburban, and rural, without having a common model.

Resource Toolbox

Grant, K. (2019). The Development of Concurrent Enrollment at The University of Connecticut. https://ece.uconn.edu/about/history/. Retrieved November 14, 2020.

Leonard, J. (2013). Negotiated Issues in an Early College Partnership: Description and Understanding through Interorganizational Theory. *Current Issues in Education*, 16(3). Retrieved from http://cie.asu.edu/ojs/index.php/cieatasu/article/view/1058.

Leadership Challenges of Early College and Dual Enrollment Programs

Staring at the nine Zoom cubes on my screen, I can tell that the discussion is not going as I expected. I had been asked to talk to the leadership of a higher education institution about early college and dual enrollment, and help them to navigate a decision that they needed to make about a curricular focus area for a new dual enrollment program. The person who invited me to the conversation is an accomplished, smart, visionary leader, but the discussion we are having today seems flat. About 20 minutes into our time together the questions turn to "will this generate revenue?" for the higher education partner. I responded that my own program certainly did not generate a profit (it was never intended to, and the program has other priorities, such as diversity). The issue of "what's in it for us" is almost always a sign that people do not buy into the concept. When it is raised, it can be a sign that people do not know enough about the model, have had a poor experience with similar programs, or are not yet in a position to move forward with the project.

A colleague of mine who has worked to support many early colleges/dual enrollment programs at the startup phase told me that to launch a successful program, the leadership at the top needs to completely buy into the program and the model – the college president and the superintendent. Then, there need to be champions at the next level down, people to shepherd the day-to-day transactions that move the program forward. Over time, more champions on campus will emerge, and also take a role in building and growing the program. But without the buy-in at the top, and the champions in the next level, any single negative decision can stop an early college or dual enrollment program in its tracks – even something as simple as where to park the school busses on campus.

The leadership component of early college and dual enrollment programs cannot be underestimated. The ability of leaders to motivate their staff to work on the programs, to recruit the right people to fill teaching and other key roles, to problem solve even when a pandemic is moving towards campus are the differences between a thriving program and a limping program, and the difference between strong outcomes for students and mediocre ones. Ironically, unlike many educational reforms that do not generate particularly good results, dual enrollment and early college programs that lose their leadership support to a retirement can be brought to a quick halt, while zombie programs with few positive outcomes can wander the landscape indefinitely.

> ## 💡 Lead to Launch:
> The Early College experience in Texas demonstrates:
> - Philanthropy and technical assistance can help launch and sustain great programs.
> - Efforts should be focused on students and communities who need the most help.
> - Leaders need to understand their community, its labor market, and which careers are in demand.
> - Programs need to be held to standards and a model to be recognized as an official early college program.

Building Early College Capacity in Texas

When you are looking for the leaders in the early college movement, people in education are often surprised that the heartland of the movement is the state of Texas. Educators often look to the two coasts for educational innovation, but the growth of early college in Texas has been nothing but, well, Texas-sized. But in Texas, leadership at the state level, and on many campuses and school districts, brought this vision to life.

In Texas, philanthropic groups and technical assistance providers helped build the field from the beginning, and shaped the way it grew and spread. From the beginning in 2005, Educate Texas and the Community Foundation of Texas helped grow early college from just a handful of schools. As Dr. Reo Pruitt of Educate Texas put it, balancing local needs and "non-negotiables" of the model was key to managing this growth.

When choosing new sites in Texas, a few key ingredients were needed. The first was having leadership who were willing to do the work that early college entailed. Next, it needed leaders who understood the job market in the region, and could design programs that would help students find their way into programs that led to a career, and not just amass college credit for its own sake. This connection to career throughout the process defines the Texas approach to early college, and is uniquely powerful to connect to first-generation students and families, particularly from immigrant backgrounds, and their families.

Building programs in Texas took many ingredients, according to Dr. Pruitt. Leadership for this effort needed to have the following characteristics:

- Leaders needed to be willing to be advocates for the program, and to get 100% behind early college.
- Leaders needed to build a culture among the teachers of high expectations, who had the same energy as the leadership to get the program moving.
- Leaders needed to be willing to be flexible in decision making – early college is not a game show, and something does not need to be a final answer. If a decision does not work, leaders need to go back and redesign or co-design.
- Leaders need to stop designing just for the next year, and to think about a whole cohort and build the support systems that students need.

Working with and in the community is critical to early college success, particularly in recruiting. Leaders have to be able to go out into the community and tell the early college high school (ECHS) story – they need to be able to tell families what ECHS will mean for the entire family, not just the enrolled student. Leaders need to be able to tell the story of how ECHS has changed the community for the better, and how it has changed educational practice.

From the beginning, the focus of early college in Texas was on the students who needed it most – first-generation, low-income students, locating many schools on the United States/Mexico border and the I-35 corridor (Laredo, Waco, San Antonio, Waco, Austin, Dallas/Ft. Worth). Pruitt emphasized that these were school districts that needed a new model and a new narrative of the education that they were offering. Early college could provide both of these for them, raising the profiles of schools while it was raising the educational achievement of students.

Building a Structure to Support your Efforts

Early colleges are, by their nature, hybrid institutions, neither entirely K-12 nor higher education in nature. When they are too much like high schools, students do not respond any differently than they do in a traditional eight-period day – which means they often pull their hoodies over their heads and wait for the last bell of the day. When early colleges just put high school students directly into a college setting without support, academic and other problems will proliferate. The leadership challenges of developing and running an early college are daunting, and the people who do this work are unique. The act of bringing together all the elements of a successful early college is a work of magic, involving economic savvy, people smarts, ability to inspire, and a gift for connecting to students and their families.

The structures that leaders build to support early colleges vary greatly by location, and can change over time. The Early College Alliance @ EMU began as a consortium of school districts purchasing space and discounted tuition at Eastern Michigan University. For years, it was a tenant and negotiated a discount for its students at the institution, then sold seats to local school districts. Over time, it evolved to have at least one EMU employee on staff, in charge of operations for the program. When the structure became too unwieldy, the ECA program evolved into part of an independent school district on three alternative programs – a degree completion program, an international baccalaureate high school. This entity had its own board, one superintendent to manage all the programs, and contracted with districts for seats in all three programs.

In Lawrence, Massachusetts, the opposite structure evolved. With a large high school and many needs, the district has built one program with a community college, and another with a four-year institution, basically forming a consortium of partners to serve its high school students. This overall structure is informal, with the two institutions beginning to build programming to meet the needs of all students in the building.

Staffing Early College and Dual Enrollment Programs

The people who work well in early college programs are not always the same as people who work well in traditional high schools. Or, as teachers transition from the traditional high school setting to the early college setting, they need to change in order to thrive, often giving up one set of roles and embracing another. As Stephen Tremaine from Bard College put it, they need to be comfortable in a role that is not either "fancy high school teacher or less fancy college teacher – something distinctive and different." Tremaine continues, "We hire faculty who have a terminal degree, have published, and who you are considering for jobs at our campus." These teachers then take on a unique role in the school, they:

> Teach students from 9th grade on – students do not meet a new group of teachers for early college. A teacher might have students for a 9th grade literature class, and then see the same teacher again for Russian literature. This makes the early college uniquely prepared to support students seamlessly. We do everything we can to replicate what defines a great college education, with small classes, taught seminar style, with support from a writing center, tutoring, and peer tutoring – everything has the feel, resources and infrastructure of a place like Bard.

People who found early colleges tend to be educators who have been looking for a new way to do things for some time. They rarely emerge from the ranks of assistant principals or headmasters, or other roles that support the current high school structure. One founder of an early college program was a computer scientist, working at the intersection of computers and education – early college was literally a way to reset the operating system of education. Another leader in the field came from the field of strategy, having worked on projects to increase the number of low-income people able to attain a college education at a reasonable cost.

Several of the first faculty at the early college were poached from positions as tutors with a local GEAR UP program. These individuals had graduated with teaching licenses, but were unable to find jobs immediately, and were working in a program to support middle school students to become ready for college. They were ideal candidates for a startup program, and had already worked in programs that aimed to build high expectations for students.

Other early college faculty were brought in from partner school districts, with the original idea that teachers might rotate through the program and bring what they learned back to their home school district. This did not work out as planned, as many teachers did not want to return to their home building, and teachers in traditional high school were not as interested in the experience of an early college program as expected. Instead, teachers who came to the early college tended to stay, adapting new roles in their new structure. One teacher who had been an English teacher and drama teacher at a traditional high school dropped the drama when she came to the early college, becoming far more focused on literature and writing.

The selection of teachers for these programs is critical, more important than any other factor. It is not an overstatement to say that early college programs could build their curriculum out of remarkable teachers and what they teach, rather than trying to plug non-ideal teachers into the system. For example, at Merrimack College we were lucky to find Dr. Michael Piatelli to teach biology in our program, and his belief in the students and his spirit have been critical to the success of the program, and who had previously had experience working with an early college effort at Boston College.

Staff who cannot be genuinely encouraging, and who cannot provide both the high standards and support needed by students, will not work well in an Early College setting. When faculty or staff are unable to get behind the project of the early college, and do not genuinely believe that students can accomplish the work, they cannot be involved – their words and non-verbal signals let students know where they stand every day. High school students have their antennae up for whether people believe in them, and will not be fooled for long. Faculty who do not believe in high expectations for all students, and that all students can meet them, ultimately undermine the program.

Scheduling: A Critical Crossroads

Early college scheduling is simply a grinding nightmare. The college schedule and the high school schedule are designed at cross purposes, and need to be meshed for a schedule to work. The two sets of calendars are different as well, so negotiating across institutions is important to harmonize the two sets of times and dates. Meredith Fitzsimmons, who manages operations for an early college, said, "Early College initiatives bridge institutions with a common goal but oftentimes very different structures, calendars and operating procedures. Opening up strong lines of communication and checking in often is imperative for the success of the program." High school schedules are designed around busses and athletics, with an early start and an early finish. College schedules are often clustered in the middle of the day, or in the afternoon, leading to a mismatch of students and available classes.

Stacey Ciprich, the founding Principal of Abbott Lawrence Academy within Lawrence High School, created a small highly diverse exam school within a huge comprehensive high school. She said that scheduling is the key to early college success, and that the work of leadership is to make sure that the high school schedule and calendar can work with the college calendar and schedule. While this may sound overly simplistic, this is actually a constant struggle, and programs that are unable to find the right times and days for college-level classes find themselves severely limited or undermined by this situation.

For our program in Lawrence, MA, we used the relatively open classroom time of 8–9:50 am to build an entire program, with students coming to campus by 8 am and leaving by 10 am. Other early college programs simply target open seats, rather than open classrooms, finding spots that are less in demand. The opportunity to rethink the schedule means that early colleges can have later start times, giving high school students more time to sleep, starting at 9 am rather than at dawn.

Either way, students expect to have some time in the afternoon for activities, particularly sports. Some early college students have turned to community teams or individual sports rather than participating in the high school sports system. Some early colleges simply have students compete with their home high school. Other early colleges use the after-school hours as prime time to offer classes that cannot be offered during the school day. Whichever direction an early college takes, scheduling and logistics will consume much of the time of school and higher education administrators.

Dual Enrollment as an Opportunity for Community Colleges

Matt Reed is America's most famous community college official, serving as Chief Academic Officer of Brookdale Community College in New Jersey, and also a prominent columnist for InsideHigherEd.com. He has written consistently about community colleges and dual enrollment/early college, extensively as a means of community colleges moving forward during a time of uncertain enrollments.

Reed's experience building early college and dual enrollment programs did not begin in a promising way. He inherited a dual enrollment program that started in the 9th grade, and was focused on getting high schoolers interested in the social sciences. This model just did not work – the 9th grade students were too immature for the college course model to work effectively, faculty did not like working with 9th and 10th graders, and students were dissatisfied that so few of the credits transferred if they left the social sciences.

The key to improving the program was to change the focus. Reed had to change the program, moving to a focus on 11th and 12 graders, and the program aimed for general education credits rather than a major. This would enable students to enter the program in 11th grade with a fighting chance to succeed, gave faculty a group of students far more mature in their classrooms, and allowed students to choose a wider range of majors, without losing so many credits at the transferring institution.

Reed views dual enrollment and early college as a way for community colleges to fight the stigma that keeps so many students from even considering a community college for their college education. If students can take a class on a community college campus (even if it is a regional campus and not the main campus) and can have a good experience with faculty there, the two-year school becomes a more viable option in their college choice. He views that as important for students across the income range. As community colleges were created to serve the whole community, Reed believes that dual enrollment and early college can help community colleges to reach both low-income students, as well as middle- and high-income students who might have looked down on the opportunity, until they have the chance to take a course while still in high school. Then, as parents talk about their students' experiences, community college gets a positive buzz in the community, for quality as well as cost.

Northern Essex Community College president Lane Glenn also sees dual enrollment as a way to break down this stigma. He told me that even within his own family, taking a class at a community college during the high school years was not an easy sell, and that one child hesitated to take the opportunity. However, as Reed had predicted, once Glenn's family members gave the community college classes a chance, they came back for more.

According to Reed, the barriers to dual enrollment and early college are numerous. The two systems have different structures, calendars, and schedules, even down to issues such as who buys textbooks. College faculty can resist the idea of being involved in a high school program, and faculty members at a community college, already feeling the stigma of teaching 13th grade, are even less likely to want to teach 11th and 12th graders. Finally, school districts each have their own funding models, leaving Reed's institution with over 30 different systems for paying for early college/dual enrollment at his single institution.

Reed believes that newer models of dual enrollment might be able to solve the problems between the systems. He is working on a system by which the high school grade for a class, and college credit, are separated. So, in a class of 25 high school history students, only 10 might be taking the class for college credit, and they would submit work to the college to be assessed for their college credits. That would put less pressure on credentials of the high school teacher, would simplify scheduling, and would allow classes to be dual enrollment classes with many fewer students than is usually needed for a section to run.

For those starting an early college or dual enrollment program, Reed advises people to be prepared to iterate as they go. With all the differences between the high school and college systems, there will always be some issue – schedules, academic support, textbooks – and be prepared to retrofit the program based on the problems that you encounter, without placing blame on either system. When a faculty member at his college found no students in his class one day because it was the day of the prom, that is no one's fault, just a problem no one had foreseen.

Lessons from the History of Early College

Graduate student Meghann Walk started her work in the field of the history of early college programs through replying to an email in her inbox. She received an email about a mid-year position at Bard's early high school in Manhattan and applied for the job. Once hired at the early college, she fell in love with the school and model.

She was not part of the first wave of faculty who founded the school, who were part of what she calls a "Wild West" of having to think through so many issues to launch the program, and the experience of wearing many hats as the school staffed up. Instead, as part of a second wave of faculty, she was able to join a high school that was an exciting place to be an educator, and to live a liberal arts ethos in a high school setting. The Bard model, unlike many others, is committed to knowledge for its own sake and living that knowledge back into the world.

Walk began writing about the history of early college when she left the Bard program to go to graduate school in education. In a history of education class, she got to choose a movement to focus on and documented the rise of the early college, from its start as an idea during World War II to its present growth. She found early college to be an interesting topic because it became a major educational reform at a time when most reforms were rooted in monitoring and accountability, where early college programs are built on optimism and trust.

She believes that the lesson on history is that early college programs can take two forms – one is trying to put together existing high school programs with college coursework – the other is using this as an opportunity to rethink the way that the whole school operates, with everyone involved thinking about what education could be.

Challenges and Opportunities for Leadership

Early colleges offer an opportunity for people to become leaders who might never be called upon to lead traditional high school or higher education programs. This leadership is often less committed to much of what makes traditional high schools tick (athletics, events) and much more focused on academics. These individuals often come from alternative programs where a focus on each student and family is the norm, and are also more analytic in their approach to academic planning and delivery. People interested in early colleges also tend to have more connections outside education – to the workplace, to industry, to community organizations – that inform their programming.

> ## ✅ The Early College/Dual Enrollment Edge: Do All Students Benefit from Dual Enrollment Programs?
>
> According to quantitative research of outcomes of dual enrollment:
>
> - All participants benefit from dual enrollment opportunities.
> - Students who are from families where they are the first to go to college see more benefits than other students.
> - Programs benefit students in terms of both high school and college completion.

What Does Research Say about the Effectiveness of Dual Enrollment

Educational researcher's Brian An's groundbreaking research on dual enrollment programs has provided the most rigorous examination of the issue of how to help low-income students best prepare for and graduate from college. Using national survey data, An teases out issues such as which students dual enrollment benefits, and how dual enrollment compares to other interventions, such as advanced placement classes, that schools often use to help raise college going rates among their students.

An was among the first researchers to systematically examine the hunch that many in the policy world had thought about dual enrollment and early college – that these interventions actually worked better with low-income and first-generation students than among their more affluent peers. This greater impact makes sense, as most middle-class and upper-class students are already aimed squarely at higher education by their family and their high school experience. As these affluent students were already on a trajectory to enter and graduate from institutions of higher learning that, frankly, were designed with their demographic in mind, dual enrollment did not provide a major boost to their enrollment and graduation rates.

As An wrote in his groundbreaking article,

> First-generation college students who participated in dual enrollment were more likely to attain a college degree than similar nonparticipants. Moreover, I found some evidence that first-generation students were more likely to benefit from dual enrollment participation than those with a college-educated parent … Overall, these findings suggest that students with college-educated parents are likely to attend college, and attain a degree, regardless of their participation in dual enrollment. Furthermore, while dual enrollment serves as a means to raise academic preparation for a wide range of students, these programs may especially benefit those lower in the socioeconomic distribution.

An's statistical approach meant that he was able to examine the statistics on dual enrollment and rather than simply compare a group of participants and non-participants, he was able to minimize the interference of key factors that could make this simple comparison misleading. An was able to compare apples to apples – low-income students who are able to take advantage of dual enrollment, to their peers who are unable to. Through this, he was able to document a small, but meaningful difference for students without parents who enrolled in or graduated college. His work is in many ways a bridge from the initial wave of enthusiasm for early college to those who sought to scale it up based on the positive results of An and other researchers.

Resource Toolbox

An, B.P. (2013). The Impact of Dual Enrollment on College Degree Attainment: Do Low-SES Students Benefit? *Educational Evaluation and Policy Analysis, 35*(1), 57–75. doi: 10.3102/0162373712461933

Walk, M. (2020). Ahead of Schedule: A History of Early College High Schools. *NASSP Bulletin, 104*(2), 125–140. doi: 10.1177/0192636520927090

SECTION

Two

Supporting and Engaging Students

 Supporting Student Learning in Early College and Dual Enrollment Programs

Even for our most talented high school students, being in a college classroom as part of an early college or dual enrollment program can be a stretch, and the jump to full-time college enrollment can be a long one. One of the top early college students at Lawrence High School (Massachusetts), Jean Espinal, took advantage of all the early college options he could, falling in love with the field of biology in the process. However, his move to Brown University as a first-year student was still an academic struggle, because of the wide scope and fast pace of his STEM course load. He found he needed to prioritize academic support, getting in contact with professors and teaching assistants from the first day of class, not even waiting for a low grade to prompt looking for support.

Dual enrollment and early college programs can produce college success only to the extent to which their graduates are prepared to navigate their relationships with professors and other support professionals, and to use those relationships to succeed. Even our top performers, on their own, are bound to struggle eventually, and those navigation skills will be critical to their classroom performance, to staying in the major of their choice, and to their college graduation.

Recruitment

In many ways, support for students in early college programs starts before they enroll. Students may not see themselves as college "material" and will need support to simply put themselves forward as a candidate for the program.

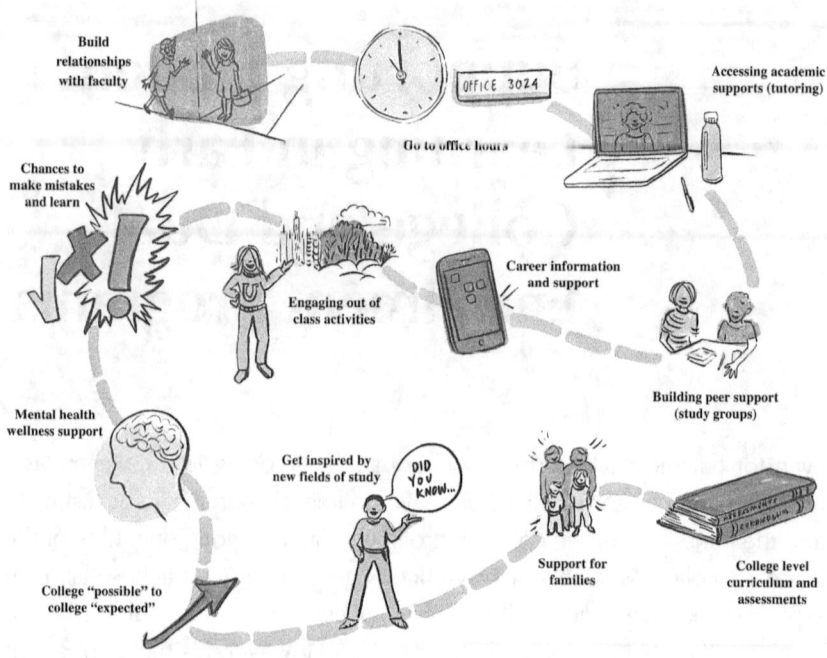

Figure 4.1 Potential student supports for early college and dual enrollment programs

Early college and school staff can assist in this process by getting the word out applying for the program broadly, and actively encouraging students to apply even when they are not positive they are ready for the experience. Without this support, research suggests that students from first-generation families, students from immigrant families, students of color, and young men will not necessarily apply, and the program will never know what it has lost out on.

Among the toughest challenges for early college and dual enrollment programs is to be able to reach out to the students who will benefit the most. Both early college and dual enrollment programs have tended to attract better educated, more affluent, and more motivated families. Building programs that represent the demographics of their community, as well as students who will truly benefit, is an ongoing challenge.

The first way to address this challenge is to identify the key places students might be coming from. In the case of Early College Alliance (ECA), in Ypsilanti, Michigan, this was middle and high schools from throughout the districts served. Recruitment nights were held, and community members gradually learned more about the resources that were available. However, ECA targeted their recruiting efforts to make sure that the free and reduced lunch rate of the student body matched the community, and that the demographics included representation of African-American and Latinx students.

Even in areas with great diversity, groups of students can be left out of recruitment. In Massachusetts, most early college students are first-generation, from low-income families and mostly immigrant backgrounds. However, English language learners can be easily overlooked because they have arrived in the U.S. in the middle of their middle or high school careers. Several programs now assess all high school students for early college potential and draw on the students in "newcomer academies," to find students whose intellectual and academic abilities are ready for early college material, but who will need some English language support to help that successfully occur.

 Lead to Launch: Kristin Hunt

Kristin Hunt has overseen early college programs in Massachusetts and believes that:

1. Early college and dual enrollment programs need to provide intentional and dedicated support services, rather than relying on tutoring or support already offered in either K-12 or higher education systems.
2. With the right level of support, many more students, and many different types of students, can find success in early college and dual enrollment programs.
3. Programs need to turn their notion of who may make a good fit for the program "upside down" and look for students that could benefit most from the program.

Rethinking who is Eligible for Early College and Dual Enrollment

Like many people in the dual enrollment and early college field, Kristin Hunt had experience working in both K-12 and higher education settings before being chosen to coordinate Massachusetts's early college initiative. She has been a leader in college access for her entire career, working in TRIO and other programs to help students pursue a college education, starting her career with work on GEAR UP in Worcester, MA. She has also worked extensively on transfer issues in higher education, giving her firsthand experience with smoothly moving students between institutions.

Hunt's office oversees and supports the full range of early college programs in Massachusetts, from two-year to four-year colleges, from state colleges to private. She identified student support as a critical area for early college success, but finds that strong programs develop intentional and specific support for early college students. In other words, programs should not make the assumption that early college students can simply be plugged into existing academic support services. Hunt notes that the key is to "break down the business as usual" approach and use early college as an opportunity to rethink how we support our students. Just expecting early college students to access tutoring services at a college, when those services might already be stretched and underfunded, is a bad idea.

The key to success in early college programs, Hunt believes, is getting everyone involved to rethink their notion of who a successful early college student might be. She offers, "You need to turn expectations upside down" and look at students who may, right now, be unengaged with high school, or not flourishing in the traditional high school curriculum and setting. These students may not "look" like college material, but the power of early college is that students who do not seem the most promising for admission to the program often are those who would make the greatest gains if they were admitted.

Admission to Early College and Dual Enrollment

Once a pool of students is recruited to apply, early college admissions can be a tricky business. In the case of both early college and dual enrollment programs, if students participate in the program and fail, they are worse off than if they had never enrolled. For instance, they end up with an F on a transcript and a real sense that they are not cut out for college at all.

However, as informed by Hunt's remarks, students should get a chance, even if their high school career to date has not been stellar. In some cases, at-risk students have responded more positively to early college and dual enrollment classes than their peers. For reasons of policy, some programs require an application, some require an assessment (usually writing and reading), while some are conducted only with a lottery of interested students.

State policies may include some admissions requirements. In Massachusetts, programs run by community colleges are required to administer the Accuplacer placement exam to potential early college students. Those who score above the cutoff are entered into the program, those below are put off to another term. The lack of equity on this system was apparent, and the Department of Higher Education allowed development of an alternative assessment– an essay and rubric that could allow a wider range of student access to early college programs.

This moment of admission is among the most important for a program, because it sets the tone for the relationship between the students, the family, the program, the school, and the college. Leslie Peralta and Niurka Aybar run the early college program at Lawrence High School, Massachusetts, and work with hundreds of students and families each year. They suggest that being clear and upfront with families and students from the start makes all the difference. When students and families enter the program with the wrong information or expectations, the relationship leads to the cases of students failing or withdrawing from the program.

Helping Students Locate and Navigate Academic Help and Support

Successful early college programs explicitly teach students how to seek help from their teachers and support systems. Students are coached on how to approach faculty members and have key conversations, such as why students are not earning the grade they desire in a class, and what more can be done. Early college alumni testify to the importance of learning how to connect to faculty and ask for help, and in academically challenging classes, such as those in STEM, they suggest that students begin to reach out for connection and help right from the start of the course, assuming that assistance from the professor and teaching assistants will be a key to success.

Early colleges, unlike traditional programs, assume that students will need, and seek, support in their college classes. When I talk to high school students, I often stress that on a college campus you need to know where to seek help before you need it. One should know where the emergency room is before you break your arm! While students hear this message, they often do not act on it with the speed that they need to, or think it applies to them. Sarah Cowdell, who is director of the Pioneer Scholars program at Merrimack College, Massachusetts, found that her early college alumni were good at reaching out to her, their academic coach, for support, but were only about as likely as the average students to take advantage of math, tutoring, or writing support on campus.

Going into an early college experience, it is important to know what support the high school staff will provide, what the college faculty will do to help during office hours, what a writing or math tutoring center can do, the difference between support for learning needs at the K-12 and college levels, and the counseling available.

🗣 Real Student: Jean Espinal

Jean Espinal is a graduate of Lawrence High School and is now at Brown University majoring in Biology. His reflections on early college include:

- Early college classes can help you fall in love with a subject, and provide ideas for you to major in in college.
- High school students need to get used to reaching out to faculty and teaching assistants early in the term.
- In high school, one can participate in a variety of activities, and often still get the course workload done. At the college level, one may have to be much more selective about student involvement depending on course workloads.

Building "Soft Skills" – the Key to Early College Success

Most of American K-12 education is focused tightly on academic skills – reading, writing, mathematics, science. However, being able to pass academic tests in these areas does not necessarily lead to college or career success. Instead, students need to be able to navigate their own learning and collaborate successfully with peers and adult supports, mirroring their future coursework and workplaces.

One key to successful transitions to freshman year and to the workforce is the concept of "soft skills." Soft skills also relate to what psychologists call "non-cognitive skills," which are the habits people develop that promote achievement. In spite of the name, research has found that non-technical skills, and non-cognitive skills, are key to success in school, the workplace, and the outside world. Anyone who has been in a workplace has witnessed smart, capable people floundering at a job, not because of a lack of knowledge, but because they could not navigate the environment or communicate effectively within the organization.

Non-cognitive or soft skills include several key factors that can make the difference between failure and success. Research has demonstrated that these are promising frameworks for boosting non-cognitive skills, and that teaching them explicitly to high school students can help them in their academic life and beyond.

Grit involves students' ability to take on difficult frustrating tasks and stick with them until successfully completed. This skill of persistence in the face of frustration can be developed, and students with all different backgrounds and circumstances already have "grit." In many cases, they need to apply it to their academic work. Psychologist Angela Duckworth's (2016) work on this topic has spurred this field forward, but it remains controversial among educators, some of whom feel that it blames students for their own lack of success.

Growth Mindset applies to students being able to understand that they can improve their abilities in an area through work, even if they have not been successful in that area in the past. This means that students believe that they can get better at a subject through effort and practice, and while they may never excel in that field, they can get the level of achievement they need to get to the next level. Carol Dweck's (2008) research on growth mindset, and how to encourage it, can help educators think about helping students be more successful, particularly by praising student effort, and not raw talent. It can also help students see that their own effort, not any limitation of their brain, controls their achievement.

Reframing Failure means helping students conceive of failure as a learning experience, rather than a label. When students are taking a class and not experiencing success, they can then learn from their experience to change their study strategy. This dovetails with helping students to be more entrepreneurial, and seeing failures as part of a longer road to success.

Helping Students Understand Their Own Learning involves giving students an owners' manual for their brain, and how to get the best results out of it. Most students reach college without much self-knowledge about how they learn, and the basics of how the brain takes the information gleaned in a lecture or textbook and turns that raw material into mastery. Many new resources have been developed to help with this. Barbara Oakley's world-famous "Learn How to Learn" Coursera is perhaps the best known, and Saundra McGuire's 2018 book, *Teach Yourself to Learn*, can help as well.

Locus of Control. Adolescents fall easily into blaming the world for their academic shortcomings. Strong early college programs stress that there are things students can control in their lives, and then focus on these. As Dave Dugger always told me, "At ECA, when things go well, it is your fault, and when things go badly, it is our fault." Helping students see that they have the power to seek out help for their classes is an important skill that will carry into their college career.

Navigating Relationships with Faculty. Sociologist Anthony Jack's (2019) study of low-income undergraduates at an elite university demonstrates that those students who could build proactive and positive relationships with faculty, through participation in office hours, were significantly more engaged and comfortable on campus. Those students who were passive or withdrawn spiraled downward, unable to access help on campus, dealing with their problems in almost total isolation. This connection with faculty can make the difference between success and failure for students, and is among the most important lessons early college alumni discuss when asked about what helped them the most.

Making Connections: The Key in Early College and Dual Enrollment

Anthony Jack's (2019) work has reshaped how people in the field view college preparation. While pre-college programs can do great work developing student work ethic and aspirations, there is more to success in college than what takes place in the classroom or lecture hall. Sociologist Anthony Jack studied students from low-income backgrounds at elite universities, and found some stark divisions. Jack terms one group of students the "privileged poor." While they came from difficult backgrounds, they had attended elite independent schools or other programs that connected them to the kind of social interactions they were expected to have in college, particularly with faculty.

Jack (2019) notes that top independent schools model college life by having faculty hold "office hours," and encouraging the development of mentor/mentee bonds between faculty and students. Thus, when privileged poor students reached campus, they reached out to faculty, visited them during office hours, and were able to navigate both the ups and downs of classwork. They successfully built relationships that resulted in opportunities as well as recommendations. These students struggled in many ways at college, but their ability to navigate this environment helped both to make the good parts of college better, and to salvage the low points of the term.

Students from poverty who went to traditional urban high schools did not have this template and struggled ever more. Jack calls these the "doubly disadvantaged," and these students made their way through a school system that rewarded staying out of trouble and keeping quiet. They scored top grades in their high schools, but were unprepared for the relationship-building they would need to do as undergraduates to be successful.

The results of these strategies, which worked so well in high school, resulted in failure on the college campus. Classwork was more difficult at the college level, but the doubly disadvantaged students shied away from office hours. Students in this group often just faded out during the term, unable to seek out help from faculty or from tutoring. They avoided letting faculty or teaching assistants know that they were struggling. As a result, they often ended up with an F for the term and might find themselves on academic probation or facing dismissal. This pattern could form a long-term spiral downward, as students become less motivated, stressed, anxious, and depressed by their failure to make good on this opportunity.

When Lawrence, MA, early college coordinator Loris Toribio worked with early college students, she focused on building programs that would build relationships between students and faculty in the junior and senior years, so that when students reached their full-time freshman year, they would have experience with a range of faculty and their relational styles. Faculty in the program were encouraged to hold office hours at the high school, coordinated with those of the high school support teacher. As a result, many students could drop in for help, to talk about the class, or to talk about their future. Results of Toribio's programming have been strong. Many of the high school students received college letters of recommendation from their college faculty, a good first step cultivating faculty help and assistance in the future.

Successful early college and dual enrollment programs explicitly use the vocabulary of "non-cognitive factors" or "soft skills" when talking to students, and it should be used across the whole staff – both K-12 and higher education. Early college and dual enrollment programs also teach academic skills and techniques more specifically than their regular high school peers, or often their college peers. Many early college programs have a set note-taking style for students, and include a notebook check for each student during the year. This might sound trivial and invasive, but taking notes, and asking questions while you read and listen, are key skills, and should not be left to the chance of the adolescent brain (Conley, 2005).

Growing from "Possible College Student" to "Expected College Student"

Michael Nakkula and Karen Foster's research is at the core of effective early college design. They studied two early college programs, one in Los Angeles, California and one in Akron, Ohio. Their work was longitudinal – that is, they and their students collected data (including interviews) on students while they were in the program, and then each year thereafter. They also paid close attention to how the students viewed themselves and their future possibilities.

When Nakkula and Foster talked to students, they found that their experience in early college reshaped who they thought they were academically, and reshaped their view of the future. For example, one student in the study entered high school thinking of applying for a city job afterwards (garbage worker), but his experience in advanced math classes (he got an A in introductory calculus in 10th grade) got him thinking instead about college and a career in engineering.

Nakkula and Foster summarize this dynamic as follows: "a psychological orientation toward college success, rooted in firsthand experiences of such success, is likely to be more realistic, more hardy, than one exclusively rooted in imagining what college will be like, based on reading about it or talking with others who have attended." This is the difference between learning from direct personal experience and trying to learn from the exhortations of teachers and other adults in your life. While not questioning the motives of the latter, it is clear that the former can be a more powerful learning experience for teenagers.

However, Nakkula and Foster found that this aspect of early college programming – being able to experience college courses, to struggle with the work, and to emerge victorious – is what makes early college such a powerful intervention. The process can move students from seeing college as the journey of a "possible self," to an "expected self." As Nakkula and Foster write, "The possible self in this regard is one that anticipates such challenges abstractly; the expected self is one that has taken on these challenges in current encounters, thereby strengthening the student for similar challenges in the future."

Most importantly, the students in an early college program develop the day-to-day skills and practices that move them towards college success. In a traditional high school, students may view their future as one of being a college student, but the habits they develop, particularly in the 12th grade, actually make this goal more remote each day. Early college students, successful or not, are faced early with college-level intellectual work, and through adult and peer support, develop strategies to overcome the obstacles and frustrations that will always be part of college-level coursework. As a result, they emerge both more skilled, and more confident, about their future path.

Real Teacher: Mary Lavallee

Mary was a teaching assistant in an early college anatomy physiology class, and her advice about tutoring early college students was:

- Teach students about the importance of review and tutoring sessions.
- Hold students accountable for attendance at support sessions.
- Teach students that academic support is part of college, from both professors and teaching assistants.

The Role of Near-Peer Teaching/Tutoring in Early Colleges

Mary Lavalee has a unique role in student support for early college – she is an undergraduate, and was a teaching assistant for the students in our Lawrence High School program who were taking anatomy and physiology last Spring. Anatomy is a challenging class, and in the section Mary worked with, it consisted entirely of Merrimack students who failed the class the previous term, plus the early college students. This is a key gateway class for students in a variety of health fields, and one's dream of nursing or another career path could perish if one fails this class.

Mary had taken anatomy in freshman year of college, and it was her favorite class. She left the first class terrified and overwhelmed, but came to love the subject matter. Her high school background, a small catholic high school, did not offer the classes that would have really prepared her for anatomy. The professor, Andrew Cannon (himself a doctor of physical therapy), would bring everything back to real life cases, even bringing in CT scans and X-rays for students to look at, to help them begin to put the puzzle pieces together.

She volunteered to work with early college students as their teaching assistant, which is a key role in an anatomy class. This class, which has an integrated lab and lecture/discussion format, involves students watching pre-recorded lectures, coming to class prepared for discussion, and then engaging in activities, including work on digital anatomy tables, as well as physical models of the human body. TAs circulate throughout the class helping students, and hold separate review hours, in which they can answer questions and go over key concepts. In classes like anatomy and physiology, this review session is key, as so much material is being taught that students can just get lost without some reinforcement and focused explanation of key concepts.

Mary felt that early college students needed encouragement to attend TA hours, which can count towards your grade in the class. Unique in our program, Mary trekked out to the high school one hour per week to hold review hours, and encouraged students to attend as much as their other activities allowed. Her main goal, besides helping them succeed in the class, was getting them used to going to TA hours and also asking the professor questions in or outside of class. The student she worked with did well in the class, better than many of the Merrimack students, and showed engagement and enthusiasm throughout.

Building Powerful Early Experiences

While not glamorous, orienting students to the early college experience is a key to their success. This needs to include both physical navigation of the campus (Where are my classes? What buildings do I need to know about?) and navigating the system (what is a registrar and where does she/he have their office?) At a minimum, students need to know where they will go each day for class, as well as about the support offices that they might need. The digital resources of the class, such as Blackboard or Google Classroom resources, are also critical for students to learn to use, and can provide early college students with a major edge once they step onto campus full-time.

Students also need help understanding the differences between high school and college classes, and the different levels of responsibility that each entails – at the college level, professors expect far more work outside the classroom than high school teachers, and do not tell students specifically when to study, but expect college students to be engaged in constant review and self-testing.

Early college students also need some fun as part of their orientation. I often build towers out of spaghetti or bridges out of index cards to illustrate points such as grit, growth mindset, or learning through failure. Rickey Caldwell, engineering faculty member, does activities such as building a race car, and connecting the design of the car to key physics principles. If college seems like an experience just like high school but with harder worksheets, students will not develop the level of engagement needed for them to be successful.

Helping Staff and Faculty Understand the College Classroom

One of the frustrating things about colleges and universities is that they are always changing, and processes that were common for previous generations may have changed greatly since. While most of your faculty and staff at a high school attended college, the ways they paid for college, registered for classes, and accessed services may have been completely different than what their students face at the present. In my own experience, college registration was still in person, in a gym, with an amazing number of physical cards to turn in. Today, registration for classes is an electronic sprint, with students assigned a time to register, then racing to get the classes they want electronically.

As a result, communication between the higher education and K-12 systems needs to include the day-to-day "how things work," systems that can be opaque to each other, as well as opaque within systems. For example, while many faculty and staff at a college know that an Access Office is supposed to support students with disabilities on campus, it was not until we had to walk early college students through the process that I learned the step-by-step system, as well as the differences between accommodations for students at the K-12 and higher education levels.

Some of the key processes to cover with early college students, staff, and even higher education faculty include:

- Differences in special education systems. Students in high school may have an individualized education program (IEP) or 504 that determines adjustments made to the curriculum. Students at the college level have accommodations to help them access course materials and assessments, but do not change the assessment itself.

- Differences in registration and adding/dropping classes. Students in high school register at the start of the year for a whole menu of classes, and only change with the help of a school counselor. Students in college make their own registration decisions, which may switch midterm. Many early colleges do not allow students at the high school level to add or drop classes on their own, due to the financial consequences of these decisions.

- Different expectations about technology. In most high schools, students are still using a physical textbook, and may be getting a photocopy worksheet or packet to complete from the teacher. At the college level, many campuses use a learning management system, and students might be expected to do reading and complete all assignments electronically. The teacher might reference these in class, but students are expected to log on and keep up with the work independently.

- Different policies. At the high school level, plagiarism and academic dishonesty often result in failing an assignment, but no other consequences for a first offense. At the college level, instructors have far more discretion about punishment – and may pursue expulsion as a penalty for plagiarism, rather than just failing the students for the assignment or asking for the assignment to be redone.

Helping Students Navigate the College Environment

Early colleges can have a different approach to tutoring than either high school or college programs. I once helped staff tutoring services for an early college program, recruiting recent graduates of teaching programs for the job. I was told that my tutors were not letting the students struggle enough, and giving them too many answers and hints. The students needed to do the work themselves, and possibly even fail the assignment, in order to learn.

This approach is closer to academic coaching than traditional tutoring. Rather than showing students how to do a type of problem, an academic coach might ask a student if they know where to start the problem – how to set it up. The coach might then just step in when the students get stuck, helping prompt next steps and ideas to try, rather than trying to manipulate the student to the right answer. This can be disconcerting, but in the long term, teaches the student problem-solving skills and strategies, rather than the answer to specific homework questions.

Tutoring and academic assistance programs tend to serve the squeaky wheels of the student (and parent) population. Students come forward and seek help, and as a result, much of the help is given to students who might not be the best candidates for it. There are A students, for instance, who regularly seek out help at tutoring and writing centers to keep their grades up, sometimes at the expense of C or D students who are less on the ball seeking help.

Early colleges need to develop systems to help identify students who need help (through progress reports or early alerts) and then to assign help to those who need it most. This might not be students who are performing in the F range – who might need to be in a different class, or may need to try the class again at a later date. Those students in the C to D range can often benefit from regular academic help, and can make strides towards better academic skills and strategies that can carry over into future classes.

To maximize success, students need to know the range of support services available on campus and at their home high school before they set foot on campus. These may include:

1. The Writing Center. One of the biggest differences between high school and college is the stress placed on writing and communication in all courses. Places that help students think strategically about their genre, audience, and argument are a key resource to make this jump.
2. Tutoring. Many campuses have centralized math, science, and other tutoring resources. In high school, this might be viewed as a sign of weakness. In college courses, use of these resources, particularly early in the term, can be a key to passing and excelling in classes.
3. Accommodations. Many students have learning challenges, often invisible. If they have a 504 or IEP, they need to work with an accommodations office to convert this to a letter for professors noting what they need for success. Getting this done early in a college career is a key to success for many students.
4. Campus Life/Dean of Students. Early college students may want to take advantage of activities run by these offices.
5. Counseling/Support. Depending on the way your early college is structured, students may want to pursue counseling through the university. Whatever your configuration of support, letting students know the importance of their own mental health and self-care is critical, as they are entering an intrinsically stressful experience.

Students Earn Privileges on Campus

While early college students are college students, they are also adolescents in high school, and need to be treated differently than traditional freshmen. The best thought out early colleges give their students some privileges to start with that go with being on a college campus, but then ask students to earn their privileges through proving their responsibility.

These can include:

Where can students go on campus? While it might seem easier to give early college students the run of the campus, this does not always work out well. On my own campus, the traditional students are about 80%

residential, and so we barred early college students explicitly from dorms. We have also held off on having students at the gym, though we have been giving students full access to the library and to the dining halls.

What events do students attend? Early college students will push to be fully a part of student life on campus. As early colleges have evolved, they are often able to find positive ways to become more a part of campus life. I have seen early college students get a tent for a football game tailgate event, for instance, to build school spirit and connection to campus. Early college students often like to be part of broader campus events, such as marches and political events. When racist graffiti was spray painted on one campus, students at the early college did a mural in response.

Working with Families

It is remarkable how difficult it can be to connect to high school students and families involved in early college and dual enrollment programs. Colleges are far more used to connecting with students than parents, and are much less likely to be proactive in reaching out. Any additional barriers, such as language, long work hours, past school issues, can make this even harder. Having staff, at the college and at the high school, who can reach out to talk to families in the language they are most comfortable in, is a key aspect of this. Having a deep cultural understanding of the families and their situation means that college and high school will not make assumptions about students and families based on their own situation, but based on the facts in the community right now.

> ### ✓ The Early College/Dual Enrollment Edge:
> Research has found that early college and dual enrollment students approach academic support differently than their freshman peers:
> - Early college/dual enrollment students are more confident.
> - Early college/dual enrollment students are less likely to seek out help on campus.
> - Early college/dual enrollment students are sometimes lost in college grading and assessment systems, which provide less frequent, less timely, and less positive feedback than their high school classes.

Differences between Early College/Dual Enrollment Students and Traditional Freshmen

Researchers have tried to examine the ways in which early college and dual enrollment students differ from freshman, especially in terms of their need for support. One of the earliest pieces in this research was carried out by Terry Born, who looked at students in two different early colleges – LaGuardia Community college in New York City, and Harbor Teacher Preparation Academy in Los Angeles, CA. Born found that students in both programs struggled with the change from the ways in which high schools supported students (reminders, extended deadlines, tutoring by teachers, frequent grade updates) and the ways college faculty conducted their classes (negative feedback, less sense of whether students are passing or not, referring students for help). Both programs responded with advising help within the program – the LaGuardia program used an advisory session run by two program staff to help students navigate the college classroom; the Harbor Teacher program used an AVID system to help students stay on top of their academic commitments.

Marvarene Oliver and her colleagues found that early high school students in grades 9 and 10 of their program had a view of support services much different than college freshman at the same institution. These early college students were entering the program with much higher confidence in their abilities (particularly in STEM fields), but with much less willingness to seek out help on campus, or as much sense that they might need help in their studies. While early college students had much less financial stress than their freshman counterparts, their overall college stress score was much higher, indicating that they were worried about the experience of taking classes on a college campus, even while they seem less likely to seek out help to address these issues. Oliver suggests that advice and support for early college students needs to be much more proactive than traditional college services, and needs to actively reach out to early college students, even to convince them that they will need help during their campus career.

Resource Toolbox

Born, T. (2006). Middle and Early College High Schools: Providing Multilevel Support and Accelerated Learning. *New Directions for Community Colleges, 2006*(135), 49–58. doi: 10.1002/cc.247

Conley, D.T. (2005). *College Knowledge: What It Really Takes for Students to Succeed and What We Can Do to Get Them Ready.* San Francisco, CA: Jossey-Bass.

Duckworth, A. (2016). *Grit: The Power of Passion and Perseverance.* New York: Scribner.

Dweck, C.S. (2008). *Mindset: The New Psychology of Success.* New York: Random House.

Jack, A.A. (2019). *The Privileged Poor: How Elite Colleges Are Failing Disadvantaged Students.* Cambridge, MA: Harvard University Press.

McGuire, S.Y. (2018). *Teach Yourself How to Learn: Strategies You Can Use to Ace Any Course at Any Level.* Stylus Publishing, LLC. Sterling, Virginia: Stylus Publishing.

Nakkula, M. and Foster, K. (2007). Academic Identity Development: Student Experiences in Two Early College High Schools. In Hoffman, N., Vargas, J., Venezia, A., & Miller, M. S. (Eds.), *Minding the Gap: Why Integrating High School with College Makes Sense and How to Do It.* Harvard Education Press. 8 Story Street First Floor, Cambridge, MA 02138 (pp. 151–158).

Oliver, M., Ricard, R.J., Witt, K.J., Alvarado, M. and Hill, P. (2010). Creating College Advising Connections: Comparing Motivational Beliefs of Early College High School Students to Traditional First-Year University Students. *NACADA Journal, 30*(1), 14–22. doi: 10.12930/0271-9517-30.1.14

Helping Early College and Dual Enrollment Students Map Their Future

Mapping out a Path to the Future

I almost always have high school students hand draw me a map from where they are now to college and a career. Some of these maps have a lot of detail and thought, and others are pretty brief. This is always an informative exercise, because it helps get the thoughts in the adolescent brain on paper, so that we can all look at the ideas together. For early college or dual enrollment students, these maps are more complex. They may be starting some college classes in high school, then moving on to college full time, then heading into the workplace. In some cases, a substantial amount of college is finished before they get there, eating into the traditional four years needed for a degree.

The research bears out this accelerated path, when you look across a large number of students. Research has shown that when you match early college students with a control group of students, you can clearly see that the early college students make progress more quickly – getting their associate's degree more quickly and graduating with a B.A. more quickly. Eventually, the most recent research shows, the control group – all students who have experienced "business as usual" high schools, do catch up. Over time, the matched students "catch up," reaching college graduation about two years later than their early college peers.

These results can either be motivational or discouraging to early college proponents. Some early college leaders were unhappy with these results. Ultimately, if early college students lose their head start, and are even with their peers by age 30, the cost and effort involved in building these programs do not look valuable. Policymakers could use this as an argument for not scaling up investment in early college, since it will not pay off more than a marginal amount over the course of a decade.

On the one hand, it is clear that early college participation can help students navigate the system more quickly, and early college students are able to surmount some curricular barriers while in high school. These two extra years can make a big difference for students and families – less money to spend or borrow, more time to get a career started, and ultimately, a quicker start on earning money from a full-time career.

There is also the case of what extra students can gain in college as a result of having extra credits. Some students might find it easier to study abroad; some may pick up an extra minor. The relief of stress from having credits should not be underestimated – this cushion of credits called a "nest egg" means that even when students might fail or have to withdraw from a class, they are still on track for an on-time graduation. Finally, early college students may choose to explore other fields, pursue internships, or otherwise deepen their experience at college, rather than cutting it short and graduating at a point educational researchers would consider "on time."

Lead to Launch: Middlesex Community College

Middlesex Community College in Lowell, MA, serves an amazing array of students from around the world. They have learned:

1. Offer early college opportunities early – as early as 9th or 10th grade.
2. Offer multiple ways for students to prove that they are ready for early college.
3. Partner with non-profit organizations that can help build capacity for the program.

Starting Early College Even Earlier

The development of a dual enrollment program in Lowell, Massachusetts, was an opportunity to bring college coursework to a diverse group of students who may not even realize the opportunities available. The Middlesex Community College program, a partnership with Lowell High School and Project Learn, brings dual enrollment programming into 9th and 10th grade, where many programs have been unable to offer classes, to help them make better-informed decisions about their coursework, future education, and eventual career.

At the start of the program, 80 freshmen at Lowell high school take a one-credit class in career exploration, to both give them a chance to try college classwork, as well as to help them focus their future dual enrollment/early college efforts. Sophomore year, students get a chance to take a college-level freshman English class, helping them to hone both their writing skills and success strategies for the college classroom. For the junior year, students need to commit to the program and plan a 12-credit program that will help lead to a major and career path. For senior year, the goal is to have more students taking classes on Middlesex Community College campus, only blocks from the high school.

Finding the teachers to work as part of the program at the high school level has been a key task. As MCC's Sothy Gaipo put in, "once teachers heard about the program they were completely invested and wanted to be a part of it." There was a lot of interest from teachers to be involved, but they needed to meet the standards for teaching at MCC, including a master's degree and professional development in the field they would be teaching in. All faculty need to be approved by MCC departments and department chairs as being equivalent to other MCC faculty. Students have also needed to qualify for the program through a 2.5 GPA, and a mix of assessments that can include Accuplacer, teacher recommendations, the PSAT, or other accepted alternatives.

MCC partnered with Project Learn, an educational non-profit to assist with the program, and the high school, community college, and non-profit partners have all worked to recruit diverse students and families to the program. Getting the word out has been important to program director Melissa Chandonnet, who said, "As a first-generation college student, I wish I had been able to do a program like this when I was in high school."

Giving Students a Voice in Program Design

When educational policymakers talk about programs such as career pathways and guided pathways, they tap into a real need for students to have a more straightforward and cost-effective education. These programs are designed to align student courses with eventual education and career goals, and to minimize course overlap, wrong turns, and dead ends that can cost students and families time and money. Early college programs have taken this model to heart, and tried to design a series of classes, taken in high school, that clear some of the key hurdles for undergraduate success.

While these are all important in early colleges, students also have a role in the design process. This is an analogue to letting a pedestrian's path help determine where to put new sidewalks – letting the user help shape the pathway. In the case of our own early college program, students' interest and success in psychology has led us to add more options to take psychology 101, and to think about ways to capitalize on their interest to present counseling as a career path for our students.

Sometimes student interest leads programs to make changes in the curriculum as well. As health care has become more important as a major/career goal to our students, they convinced us to add Anatomy and Physiology I as an early college offering, despite its difficulty and its high college student failure rate. The 12 students in the class had a 3.04 GPA average, and while the course was a challenge for all of them, they embraced this challenge, spending an extra session per week with a teaching assistant at the high school who came over each week for a review session.

🗣 Real Student: Paul Akande

Paul Akande is an alumnus of Washtenaw Technical Middle College and is from Ypsilanti, Michigan. He now works for a major petroleum company as an engineer. He draws these lessons from his education and career:

1. Early college programs can help students develop a sense of personal responsibility that will help them in school and their career.
2. Early college students do not always need extensive sports or activity programs – they can create their own recreation opportunities.
3. Students need to have motivation and grit to stick with STEM career paths – but it is worth it in the end.

I met Paul Akande when he was just graduating high school from Washtenaw Technical Middle College (WTMC), located in Ann Arbor, Michigan. He was on his way from WTMC to the University of Michigan School of Engineering, and I helped him get some scholarship money that was due to him as an alumnus of an Upward Bound program for Ypsilanti, Michigan. Even back then, Paul was a serious young man intent on a career in engineering.

Paul had applied to WTMC as a result of the influence of his family. He had not heard much about the program, but once he heard what it offered – the chance to complete high school with as much as an associate's degree worth of credit by high school graduation, he was sold. He first chose a graphic design track, then switched to a general math and science track. While he missed some social aspects of high school, he played ultimate frisbee for WTMC and did not feel any lack of social or athletic life in his time there.

He credits WTMC with both solid coursework and with teaching him about personal responsibility for his own education. Unlike a traditional high school, WTMC put the emphasis for success on the student, and challenged students to take this seriously. As a result, when Paul got to the University of Michigan, he viewed his success as his own responsibility, and when larger classes did not have an attendance policy, Paul still attended, making sure he was giving the class his all.

At the University of Michigan, Paul found the coursework different than what he was ready for. He found that he needed to retake a few of the introductory college-level STEM courses in a format with calculus, in order to have the foundation he would need for upper level classes. He briefly even toyed with leaving engineering for computer science, but decided to stick with engineering for the career opportunities it presented. While he did not feel his transition to college-level STEM was completely smooth, he never felt as though he was in danger of not being able to complete a STEM major at Michigan.

With some summer internship experience he gained as a student at Michigan, he took a job with a major energy firm and moved to Houston after graduation, where he still lives. He is grateful for the opportunities that majoring in a STEM field have given him, and he feels that now that he has a career, he can return to interests in areas such as video editing and production that he considered in high school.

Transferring Credits: The Thrill of Victory and the Agony of Defeat

The Achilles' heel of dual enrollment or early college programs is the credit transfer process. This is the piece of the process that the early college program has little control over, and even whole state university systems have trouble regulating. In a perfect world, early college credits would transfer seamlessly, much like other college credits should (such as those from community colleges). Since institutions of higher education are all accredited and certified by both state and nationally-recognized bodies, there should be no real reason for a class offered at one campus to not transfer to another.

However, even colleges and universities that purport to support affordability and transferability of credit can refuse to accept credit at all, or accept them only as an elective credit, not counting towards general education or the major. Colleges can offer a wide variety of reasons for their decisions, some making more sense than others. Among those I have been given to reject my college's credits include: where the class is taken (high school or campus), who else is in the class with the student (other high school students or college students), who is teaching the class, the textbook used, the syllabus, the topics covered, and the tests given. All of these reasons really just boil down to "no," and colleges with early college programs will need to invest time convincing other colleges to actually accept their credit, through sheer perseverance – offers to drive over and talk about the issues in person seem to help the most.

The ultimate question about credit transfer is simply "are we leaving the student back?" Just like with military students and transfer students, the system should not make students retake materials that they have already had, and have shown that they have mastered through class assessments. More than the costing money or time to degree, making people sit through a class they have already passed is disrespectful, and creates students who are frustrated from the start of their education in the new institution.

Colleges can put up barriers for dual enrollment students without even trying. Stacey Outlaw's dissertation on early college students demonstrated that the university's surcharge on college credits earned over the 124 needed to graduation added a layer of problems for early college students, who may have entered with 60 credits, but who may have needed classes in majors and minors that tools them over 124. This surcharge, which could be an additional 40% on tuition, was eventually forgiven for many early college students, but did not apply to AP or IB credits, penalizing students who transferred in with early college or community college credits.

Admission and Financial Aid

Getting colleges to take early college and dual credit programs seriously starts with the admissions process. Admissions is the key office of a college in terms of who gets admitted (and who gets rejected); they often manage the transfer credit process, and can give students a good idea of what may or may not be possible in terms of credits. As colleges become more involved in early college and dual enrollment programs, they will hopefully become more enthusiastic in their recruitment of students who earn these credits and bring them to campus. Since colleges need to accept their own credits, early college and dual enrollment is a powerful form of student recruitment, often yielding a stronger academic background and more diverse applicant pool than the college's traditional admissions funnel.

Financial aid can take many forms for dual enrollment and early college students. The first form of financial assistance is just accepting the maximum number of credits, and giving credit in the major or for general education. This can cut college costs by 16–30% for many students. Colleges can also offer scholarship programs for early college participants – my college has been offering up to 10 full scholarships for students who are graduates of our early college program, an amazing offer that includes room and board and money for books. Programs such as Posse and QuestBridge have also leveraged students' early college or dual enrollment experiences into offers of admission and scholarships from top schools.

At the highest levels of selectivity, such as Ivy Leagues, colleges may simply not offer credit for anything, but the level of financial aid given can more than offset this disadvantage. For many students, a chance to spend four years at a top institution, often emerging debt-free, can be more important than getting their AP or early college credit. In fields such as STEM, taking the AP class or introductory class at a local college can give you a fighting chance in the gateway STEM coursework, where those without this leg up will simply be washed out into other majors. Early college or dual enrollment programs that have a pathways model can help build these gateway classes into the high school experience, allowing students to enter college at least one hurdle ahead in their major – our program added Anatomy and Physiology to our program to allow health science students a leg up in their studies.

Bottlenecks in the System – Advising, Transfer Processes, and Campus Climate

Research on the experience of early college students once they get to a four-year campus shows a mixed picture of the results. In many cases, students' credits may not transfer in the right way, or may not fit with the way that the major is structured. Further, if the four-year college has a weak advising system, students can get lost on their way to their degree. Stacey Outlaw's research on early college students on the campus of a four-year research university showed that many of her subjects failed to connect with their advisor at college, and received far less time and attention for advising than they had in the early college program.

Outlaw also found that the students she studied encountered a range of racial harassment on campus, as well as pressures related to being minority students at a primarily white institution (80%). Students in her study reported feeling ostracized and marginalized at events, especially football games, and encountering negative attitudes towards African-Americans in many circumstances. The campus culture itself was difficult for many of her subjects to deal with, as it was based on language and imagery from the Confederacy. This clash of students and the social milieu of their college can lead to terrible outcomes, as the students may be more than academically qualified to attend and succeed at the college, but find the college campus so socially problematic that they may leave college or transfer their credits to another institution.

New Ways to Think about the Connection between Education and Careers

When I started as a GEAR UP director in 2006, I thought a lot about college application and acceptance as a "finish line" for students. Time and hard experience with my students has shifted my thinking on this issue. I no longer regard getting a "fat envelope" in the mail senior year from a college as the finish line for high school – it is really just a start. If you work backwards from a first job in your profession as the goal, then academics and career/professional education form a single braid. Professionals in education talk more about "work-based learning," in which students start to see what is taking place in a career or profession well before they start. This form of education also shows students the skills needed in their field, answering the question "why do I need to know this" with firsthand experience watching professionals in the field use those skills.

 ## College and Other Options

At the end of their time in an early college program, students face different choices than traditional high school students. They often have at least 12 to 16 college credits earned in real college classes, and need to choose whether to stay with the college with which their early college is affiliated, or switch to a new environment.

Unfortunately, colleges and universities can be less than helpful in transferring credits. Transferring credits between two- and four-year institutions can be tricky, and sometimes even four-year institutions are not happy to accept credits from rival colleges. Idiosyncratic general education systems do not help either, as some colleges (such as mine) are looking for a specific theology class for their students.

For many students, staying at their present college makes the most sense. They have learned the system, the institution is often close to home, and there is a clear path to graduation. This is one of the main reasons higher education institutions become interested in dual enrollment or early college programs – getting amazing students in the process. For other students, negotiating a path beyond this institution, even if it means not getting all the credit for their work, makes more sense. As higher education becomes more familiar with early colleges, and the advantage that the students bring, they will become more enthusiastic recruiters of these students, who have a higher propensity to succeed and graduate than traditional students.

Other Paths: the Armed Forces, Gap Year Programs, Career Programs, and Community Colleges

Early college students have options beyond that of the traditional four-year college after they graduate. Many students and families are deterred by the cost of a traditional four-year residential college experience, or have family needs that preclude heading out of state to a distant college campus. Community colleges are often the hosts of early college programs, and serve as the destination for many graduates. These often have a combination of solid academics for those who wish to transfer to a four-year school, as well as career programs that can lead to a good career. The low cost of attendance, and the lack of a need for loans, make these schools increasingly attractive, particularly for Latinx students and families.

Given the maturity level of many students, a "Gap year" has become more popular. As many students are finishing senior year of high school without clear ideas of what to do in the future, taking a year to work or volunteer makes a lot of sense, and is becoming more accepted as a path on the way to college.

There is a new expansion of work-based education programs, or apprenticeships, outside the skilled trades that traditionally host them. Institutions such as banks and credit unions see an opportunity to work with students as they are exiting high school to learn about the banking industry, and then have those young people pursue a degree once working for the bank. This allows the bank to find long-term employees, and to help reduce the amount of student loan debt that these students might carry. Health care organizations are also seeking more programming to help fill entry level positions, and then help employees increase their educational level while on the job.

Students also look to programs or opportunities to pay for schooling. Programs such as AmeriCorps and City Year can provide an educational benefit for participants and graduates, as well as providing amazing experiences and growth opportunities for young people. While taking time off between high school and college is still countercultural in the United States, these experiences can help students mature a bit before entering a full-time freshman year.

Other students seek out military opportunities, as the revised GI Bill provides for educational benefits both for the enlistee, and potentially for their family members. While the military is not always a choice considered equivalent to going to college, for many students it provides a structure and resources that can help them start a career.

> ### ✅ The Early College/Dual Enrollment Edge:
> Research in North Carolina's sprawling network of early colleges has shown us that even when students are randomly admitted to an early college, they thrive relative to their peers who do not attend. Dr. Edmunds's research shows:
>
> - Early college students all benefit from the programming, while students from lower income brackets benefit the most.
> - Early college students pursue their studies both to move ahead more quickly and to save money for themselves and their families.
> - Early college students now tend to be more students who do not fit into their high school, than those who are academically below average.

Dr. Julie Edmunds and Early College Achievement

Dr. Julie Edmunds was in the right place at the right time to research early colleges and their impact. Right as she was finishing up her Ph.D. she was brought on board by a research center to provide evaluation support for the New Schools Project, a public–private partnership that sought to change the way North Carolina did high school. At the time, there were two paths forward – one, an early college model that would help high school students access college classes; the other, breaking large high schools into a series of smaller schools, usually organized around a theme (environmental science, STEM, arts).

Dr. Edmunds became more deeply involved in early college work, and seeing the growth in demand, offered the schools to conduct their lottery process for them to choose students, while tracking data on both the students who ultimately enroll, and those who are turned away. Thus, Edmunds created the first and longest lasting longitudinal and random control early college study, based originally on the 12 schools who let her center run the lottery process.

Since those beginnings, Edmunds and her colleagues have been able to track high school achievement, high school graduation, college enrollment, and college retention/graduation, and are working on ways to track the income levels of students when they enter the labor market. It is Edmunds's work that has gone the furthest to proving that early college programs can work for all students, even though she readily admits that students who enter the lottery for early college are more motivated than their peers in comprehensive high schools.

Early colleges, in Edmunds's research, have proven to help students on every variable measured, except for English/Language Arts confidence. Originally, Edmunds thought that early college programs would benefit students towards the bottom of the academic class more, but that has not yet shown up in the research. Instead, the model has attracted the "blue haired kid" who is not fitting in at the traditional high school, but will respond to the opportunity and smaller setting of an early college program. As they move forward, low-income students tend to see the most benefit from early college programs, as they embrace the opportunity to move forward with as many credits as possible, and to reduce their costs once in college.

Edmunds believes in early college and dual enrollment as not just a way to get credits, but also as a way of rethinking high school, and creating smaller, more intentional, communities that truly encourage students to engage. She believes that early college is a "wedge" for a broader reimagining of high school, with changes in instruction, the faculty role, and the relationships within the school.

For some students, dual enrollment and early college might be a way to advance towards the workforce more quickly, and to have a head start on gaining a credential, or a two- or four-year degree. Dr. Edmunds sees work on career academies in North Carolina as part of this movement, which could reach a different audience than dual enrollment programs that are focused on getting students into and through four-year colleges, often with expectations of further academic work to come.

Resource Toolbox

Edmunds, J.A., Willse, J., Arshavsky, N. and Dallas, A. (2013). Mandated Engagement: The Impact of Early College High Schools. *Teachers College Record, 115*(7), 1–31.

Edmunds, J., Unlu, F., Furey., J, Glennie, E., and Arshavsky, N. (2020). What Happens When You Combine High School and College? The Impact of the Early College Model on Postsecondary Performance and Completion. *Educational Evaluation and Policy Analysis, 42*(2), 257–278.

Outlaw, S.E. (2017). Early College High School Participants' Transition to a Research University. [Unpublished doctoral dissertation]. North Carolina State University. https://repository.lib.ncsu.edu/bitstream/handle/1840.20/33604/etd.pdf?sequence=1, Retrieved November 14, 2020.

Vargas, J. (2019). Breaking the Boundaries between High School and College: How to Scale Success for Low-Income Students. Boston, MA: Jobs for the Future. https://files.eric.ed.gov/fulltext/ED598372.pdf. Retrieved November 14, 2020.

Building Powerful STEM Experiences for Early College/ Dual Enrollment Students

Science, Technology, Engineering, and Mathematics (STEM) majors are among the most in demand for colleges and in the workplace. Graduates in STEM fields, such as engineering, biology, or physics make a premium of 30% over college graduates in other fields. As a result of the perceived gap in the number of young people entering STEM fields, there has been a great deal of interest in early college and dual enrollments focusing on creating pathways that can ease student transition from high school to college to career, with STEM areas at the center of these. Part of this demand comes from students and parents themselves, who see starting salaries and employment numbers for STEM and health care areas, and want to prepare to pursue those jobs. However, for STEM graduates without soft skills, the ability to communicate clearly, and leadership aptitude, this bonus can fade out, leaving the engineer earning less than a liberal arts peer in a few years in the workforce. As a result, when building a STEM program for early college and dual enrollment, the design of the program should focus on the long term, rather than the first job starting salary. There are key skills and classes that can truly give students seeking a STEM degree a better chance of being able to pursue that field successfully.

First among these is mathematics, which can keep many students out of STEM fields altogether. Particularly for students from less advantaged backgrounds, getting a good start on mathematics in high school can help them avoid the remedial classes that spell the doom of many aspiring STEM majors. Getting through some calculus before high can make a real difference for students and can put them on an equal footing with their peers. Next are foundational classes in areas such as the life sciences. Our students have done well in biology, with a focus on genetics, in our early college program. These courses, taught at the college level, connect to many areas that students are interested in, such as health care and medical treatment, as well as to issues in their own lives, such as the spread of diseases.

Classes that are foundational in the health sciences have also proved popular with students in our program. For our seniors, we added anatomy and physiology, long the bane of students in health science and nursing. While a challenging class to tackle in high school, those students who pursue this path will enter college able to start with classes that do not serve as gatekeepers for their field.

Laboratory coursework is a unique challenge for early college and dual enrollment programs. Many students in urban settings enter high school without the lab science background that many instructors take for granted. Many high schools look to early college or dual enrollment opportunities to fill in opportunities that are hard to get in the regular high school curriculum due to facilities and cost. However, helping students understand topics such as lab safety, lab procedure, data analysis, and lab report writing is a tall order, often only tackled in one session per week.

Researchers have found that STEM classes are often the toughest part of early college to get right, in part because the college classes that they draw on are often difficult and not organized with an eye to student success. In her article "Early College High Schools: Lessons Learned in the College Science Classroom," Adrienne Alaie discussed the difficulties of teaching early college students in the context of a large (700+ student) biology lecture class. Of the 37 early college students enrolled in the class, few attended lectures and separate early college recitation sections, very few passed the midterm exam, and only a handful passed the final exam and the class. The author argues that the disengagement of the students led them to fail, and that as a result, they lost motivation to take STEM coursework in the future. This left the students in the early college program worse off than if they had delayed their STEM experience until freshman year (Alaie, 2011).

Lead to Launch: William Leach

William Leach is the Principal of the STEM/Engineering Early College at the University of North Carolina – Charlotte. To build powerful STEM programs he suggests:

- Offer as much coursework as you can before students take first year STEM and engineering college classes.
- Offer maximum support to students in the early years of their time in early college to build their skills before they enter the college classroom.
- Be open to students not pursuing STEM careers and majors – they will use those problem-solving skills wherever they go.

Early College Programs that Focus on STEM

William Leach is not your average early college principal. With 21 years of experience in traditional high schools and middle schools before moving into leadership in early college, Leach drew on his traditional school experience to build an innovative STEM/engineering early college at University of North Carolina – Charlotte. He compares his engineering early college (in its sixth year) to a middle school model – a holistic approach to student achievement and support, a focus on career/academic exploration, grade level teams working together on curriculum, and a commitment to helping every student meet their own goals.

His Engineering Academy is located on the campus of UNC-Charlotte, and his 350 students have an option of a 5th year of early college, which amounts for most to be a free full year of college classes at UNC-Charlotte. His students are graduating, and moving on to college either at UNC-Charlotte or other colleges or trade schools, and as they move into the college classroom, respect for the program grows across campus.

Focus on Teaching the Students You Have

The biggest obstacle STEM and engineering early colleges face is working with the students who arrive on campus freshman year. For Leach, this means whichever students have applied to the school and passed through a lottery process. These students attended a range of schools before this, and their performance, particularly in key areas such as math, can range from top of the class to remedial. But Leach views this policy as a strength, as the school has become representative of the district's demographics, and with the addition of free bussing from anywhere in Charlotte, is accessible to more students and families than ever. He says "We will take all comers," and he is proud of that distinction.

The school program is designed to engage students from day one, and to connect engineering and STEM to whatever students may want to pursue in the future. Students take an array of classes at the early college, including math, project lead the way engineering curriculum, and other key STEM subjects such as chemistry. Unlike many other programs, much of the high school coursework is not dual credit, by design. The students need that coursework, particularly in areas such as English and writing, to eventually succeed in key gateway classes offered on campus. By junior and senior year, students are taking more classes on the UNC-Charlotte campus, and in the fifth year, students begin the engineering sequence.

The program does not work for every student, and by sophomore year, the school might be having hard conversations with students about their achievement – whether having a 2.4 GPA at the school will ultimately lead to the kind of college admission that the student and family might expect. Graduates of the program do not all go on to engineering, either. Many graduate from the engineering early college and pursue other fields in STEM, such as computer science, or areas of the social sciences, such as criminology. Leach believes that these students still gain from the curriculum, particularly skills such as design and problem-solving, and bring these with them into new fields.

The classes at the school are designed to be engaging, with little teacher lecturing or talking. Students are formed into teams, working around tables rather than desks, and classrooms hum with the noise of student discussions – the classrooms look more like elementary classrooms in their setup than traditional high school rows of individual desks, with only 20 to 25 students per class. Leach has focused on finding teachers who are seasoned, but are open to the model, and finding good math teachers has been a key to the program's success.

Leach sees the big advantage of early college being access and affordability. Particularly with the 5th year free, students are able to take advantage of a range of options that other programs do not have. Some students are graduating the program with 70 college credits, making them over halfway done with a rigorous academic program. In that 5th year, the students continue to receive support through the school, attending a seminar, and receiving help with the college applications process.

The students have made a name for themselves at UNC-Charlotte and beyond. The average GPA of the students in college classes has been 3.0, quite an achievement in many STEM classes. UNC-Charlotte and other colleges have ramped up recruiting his students, and Duke Energy just announced the funding for scholarships for eight students per year to attend UNC-Charlotte to provide funds for early college students to finish their program at UNC-Charlotte for free.

Still, the program has not reached all the students it could, according to Leach. "I wish I could go out and recruit more diamonds in the rough," Leach says, and when he goes out to middle schools to recruit, too many students and families tell him that they had never heard of the school until they met him. Leach is most proud of students who came into the school disengaged, and went on to achieve: "we have students who would not have made a high school diploma in a traditional high school." Through the support and engagement of the program, they graduated and went on to college, even if it is not in a STEM area.

Connecting the early college to the engineering and STEM curriculum and faculty at the college level has been the biggest challenge. Some college leaders simply never set foot in his building to learn more about the school. Others felt that the students would not be able to handle the work once they got to campus. Space has been a constant challenge, and next year, 9th graders will be in another building as a result of the space crunch. However, with six classes in engineering before they arrive at their first college-level engineering class, the students have performed well once they reach college engineering courses. However, the "gatekeeper" nature of STEM and engineering classes, with the built-in notion that many students will fail, creates an atmosphere in which students choose to not pursue engineering, or even STEM, out of dislike of the atmosphere.

Connecting High School Students to College STEM Experiences

Kaitlin Dinet has worked supporting students in the Merrimack College/Lawrence High School program from the start three years ago. She graduated with her Master's Degree in 2017, and took the position at Lawrence High School in order to work closely with college faculty on a new early college program. She credits her mentors at the college and the high school with helping her make the jump from teaching middle school to supporting high school/college classes.

Dinet works with the high school students on the days they are not on the college campus to make sure they are getting all the information they need for their high school state curriculum and exams, and to keep them making progress on their college coursework. She works to make sure all students are ready for the college-level coursework, even when their elementary and middle school backgrounds are uneven, and not preparing the students completely for the coursework they are taking. The high school, over time, has built a talented staff of STEM teachers, and worked to curriculum map backwards from the college curriculum, to build excellent 9th and 10th grade physics and chemistry curriculums.

Dinet works with the college faculty member to support students. They meet in person once a week, and talk by phone constantly. This includes looking at the data on student achievement, looking at ways that both of them are teaching, and keeping on the same page. This work supports the students, who Dinet describes as

> amazing – the kids really love to learn, and they are just coming to biology. They want to learn, they enjoy the process of learning science, and they love having a choice in their assignments, and they love the real-world applications of science.

The biggest barrier to getting students interested in STEM, according to Dinet, is discouragement they have received in earlier grades or experiences, that makes them feel like they are "not STEM people." Even if students come into the class with significant gaps in knowledge, all of that can be filled in between the high school class, the college lecture, and the college biology labs. Once students have successfully finished their first college biology class "the gains of being in the class are huge. Even though the class is only a few months, the gains they make are huge. They are way ahead – thinking like a scientist, being in the laboratory."

The way that STEM classes transfer into colleges can make a big difference for students in fields such as STEM, arts, or architecture – any field that has substantial laboratory or studio components. Unlike in the case of social sciences or humanities, early college students can find their transferable credits eating up their elective opportunities, leaving them with a schedule that might comprise all upper level classes with substantial time commitments. Dr. Bradley Smith's dissertation, a qualitative study of early college students to a four-year university, demonstrated that STEM and other time-intensive majors were an imperfect fit with the early college curriculum, leading to frustration over the credit load and sheer difficulty of the first terms of full-time college. Particularly if students were fully committed to graduating early, this could lead to an unbalanced schedule, much different than that of their age-peers on campus, and could lead to lower GPAs than their peers due to the sheer difficulty of the work.

🗣 Real Student: Simonai Santiago

Simonai was a star student in her high school in Lawrence, Massachusetts and attended Holy Cross University in Worcester, MA. Her advice for aspiring STEM students is:

1. Form study groups immediately in your classes. Those people will become both your support and your friends.
2. Watch how many tough STEM classes you take at a time. Because of transfer credits, you may lose out on some of the electives that can break up a killer schedule.
3. Be ready to navigate academic support and especially office hours with professors and teaching assistants.

The STEM Path for Early College/ Dual Enrollment Students

Simonai Santiago was one of our standout early college students in Lawrence, and has made her way to College of the Holy Cross University in Worcester, Massachusetts. She fell in love with biology in her junior year class with Dr. Michael Piatelli and is now studying health studies (an interdisciplinary major).

A few key elements of the early college program helped her get a jump on STEM. The mix of lecture, discussion, and case studies in her biology class helped her develop study skills in the field. Through the early college program she was already used to developing a relationship with the professor through office hours: "I knew the story, I knew how this goes. Going to office hours was seamless for me. I was not afraid to talk to professors." Her coursework at Merrimack and her high school helped her get ahead in her program. Taking a full year of calculus, including a semester at Merrimack, helped her in math. Her AP class in chemistry helped her be prepared for chemistry at the college level. Taking government at Merrimack meant she could skip it at Holy Cross. Holy Cross was accepting of some credits and resistant to accepting others – my offer to stop by and talk to them about credits did prompt them to accept biology credit.

However, the first year was a struggle. At Merrimack, she took one class per term, and at Holy Cross, taking three STEM classes in a term was a lot for her to manage. Classes were difficult, and though Simonai persevered, she did switch her major from a biology/pre-med track to health studies, an interdisciplinary program that combined science and social science.

Based on her experience with her cohort at ALA, Simonai immediately began forming study groups at Holy Cross, and through doing this made friends with people in similar majors. As Holy Cross is a Predominantly White Institution (PWI), having this group of peers to connect to helped Simonai develop a good social network.

Simonai's experience of freshman year represents what can be positive and frustrating about applying the early college experience once students are in college full time. On the one hand, all the background and preparation cannot prepare for every college class, and particularly the full load of courses, living away from home, and fitting into a new social life. While the experience and credits of early college can keep students from falling down freshman year, it does not always mean that they are able to attain their own ambitions for themselves, and they still may need help navigating their next steps.

> ### 🗣 Real Teacher: Shannon Morey
> Shannon is a Knowles fellow and physics teacher at Abbott Lawrence Academy. She teaches students in grades 9 to 12, and has taught them mathematics, chemistry, and physics. Her advice to prepare students for STEM success is:
>
> - It is important to keep students motivated and excited about STEM, and not to discourage them about their abilities.
> - Teaching students teamwork and group work skills takes time, but is important to their long-term success.
> - College STEM classes need to change to become more active and engaged, so that students do not become discouraged with their gateway classes and continue in their majors.

Encouragement, Motivation, and STEM

Shannon Morey, a physics teacher in Lawrence, Massachusetts, remembers her own STEM experiences in high school and college when she thinks about the students she is teaching. She said,

> I myself did not have a lot of STEM opportunities in my small rural high school. We had only two AP classes that I could take. The first term of college I realized I did not have the experience that other students had doing labs or writing lab reports. I had to work 10 times as hard that term to keep up.

However, she believes that unequal background is not the top problem in STEM, but encouragement motivation. She said,

> When I teach students in 9th grade physics, I have to deal with a wide range of skills. But the main problem can be their experience with science. If they have had teachers who encouraged them in science, I can teach them skills, like determining a slope. But if they had a bad experience in STEM classes, and

developed a mindset that they were not "STEM material," it is much harder to turn that around.

To get students ready for college classes, whether early college classes or their first year of full-time college, Morey works on a few key skills: how to work together as a team, and to observe the key norms of my classroom. This is part of the practice of complex instruction, which she learned as part of the Knowles fellowship, and implemented in her classroom.

Morey believes that colleges themselves need to change to allow more students to thrive in STEM majors and classes. She said,

> For more students to be successful, college classes need to become more supportive for students. We put the onus of seeking out support on the student, instead of building a classroom that supports them throughout, and that uses techniques like active learning rather than lecture and PowerPoint. So, we need to work on our students' self-advocacy skills so they can get the help they need, but we also need to create the classes where students can be more successful.

✓ The Early College/Dual Enrollment Edge:

Research on STEM students in early college reveals:

1. There can be a major dip in satisfaction for students in their first year of college-level STEM classes.
2. This dip eventually goes back up, and students are as satisfied as their freshman level peers.
3. Students in these programs make great gains in self-efficacy and seriousness, key areas for long-term success as adults.

The U-shaped Experience in a STEM Early College

Educational researcher Michael Sayler looked at the data generated by the 25-year history of the Texas Academy of Math and Science, founded in

1987 at the University of North Texas. These students, unlike almost all the rest in this book, took a leap of faith to leave their families and live on campus (in separate dorms) for 11th and 12th grade on a college campus. These students took college-level courses in math, science, and other STEM fields from the start, in the same classes as college freshman and sophomores.

Students in the program were adapting to many different changes through this program – they were living away from their families, they were taking college-level classes, and they were in a peer group that both shared their interests, but were also as academically talented as they were. Thus, students found themselves moving from a situation where they were top math students in their high school to one in which they were in the middle of the pack (or lower) in competitive classes and fields.

Sayler, reviewing the research and data, found that students in the program had an initial dip in feelings of self-esteem and well-being. Sayler wrote, "Over the first year of college, the TAMS students in this study experienced less satisfaction with what they were achieving in life, less satisfaction with personal safety, and less satisfaction about their future security." However, these STEM students then began to rebound:

> In a study of TAMS students, 1 to 5 years after leaving TAMS (Boazman & Sayler, 2011), the average overall well-being was statistically the same as the level of personal well-being found in TAMS students at entrance to the program. They specifically reported elevated levels of satisfaction in their achievements, immediate standard of living, personal safety, and future security than age peers. They expressed powerful feelings of general self-efficacy and high levels of trait seriousness, two constructs related to facilitating success.

Resource Toolbox

Alaie, A. (2011). Early College High Schools: Lessons Learned in the College Science Classroom. *Urban Education, 46*(3), 426–439. doi: 10.1177/0042085910377847

Boazman, J. and Sayler, M. (2011). Personal Well-Being of Gifted Students Following Participation in an Early College-Entrance Program. *Roeper Review, 33*(2), 76–85.

Deming, D.J. and Noray, K.L. (2018). *STEM Careers and Technological Change*. Cambridge, MA: National Bureau of Economic Research.

Sayler, M.F. (2015). Texas Academy of Mathematics and Science: 25 Years of Early College STEM Opportunities. *Roeper Review, 37*(1), 29–38. doi: 10.1080/02783193.2015.975773

Smith, B.M. (2019). *From Early College to the University: A Case Study Exploring First-Semester Experiences* (Doctoral dissertation, The University of North Carolina at Charlotte). North Carolina: Charlotte.

Opening Doors for Students
Social Sciences in the Early College/Dual Enrollment Programs

One of the big mysteries of early college and dual enrollment programs is why students gravitate to certain fields of study, and are repelled by others. Unlike traditional college majors, students in an early college are often truly undecided, and truly exploring the curriculum, not yet focused on a job or a graduate/professional school. One day, walking across campus, I ran into one of our early college students as he was leaving class. He was just finishing up this "Introduction to Engineering" class. I asked him what he was enrolled in the next term: "Psychology. I need to know engineering, but I also need to know myself."

Social Sciences as a Way of Learning about the World

There is an enormous gulf in the way social sciences and history are taught and studied in high school and in college. High school history and social studies teaching is usually mocked as the great depression scene from the movie *Ferris Bueller's Day Off* ("Anyone? Anyone?", the bored teacher asking over and over), which is certainly an overstatement of the problems of the field. But students often arrive at a college classroom with an idea of history that is names and dates, and little sense of what social science is or what social scientists do. Even Advanced Placement classes, which were designed to give students a taste of college-level work, are often exercises in information processing, rather than critical thinking or research.

Strong early college and dual enrollment programs try to bridge this gap, especially by looking ahead to the powerful experiences students can have in college in these fields. The best early college teachers in history and social sciences are able both to give students a taste of what is to come, as well as to teach them the material and skills that will be needed to get there. This is a balancing act, because history and social science fields build on a certain amount of rote learning, and involve some key skills (reading, note-taking, writing) that need to be done in order to learn fully from the types of active learning, simulations, and debates that make the field engaging at the college level. But in fields such as the social sciences, without big salaries to lure students, the teaching and activities need to grab students, and hold on for the full term.

Real Student: Emely Siri

Emely Siri enrolled in Bennington College in Vermont, after graduating from Lawrence High School in 2019. She identified these lessons from her experience:

- Early college classes provide a good preview of college level classes, where the faculty member may seem more distant than high school teachers, but are important to connect to.
- Being in college classes with "regular" undergraduates while still in high school gives you confidence, especially when your high school is culturally different from the population of the college.
- Early college teaches you to focus on what you are learning, not what the people sitting around you may think about you.

The Value of Psychology, Political Science, and History

While students often enter our classes with a strong sense that STEM classes can help them succeed in the future, they are not always aware of what history and the social sciences can do for them. In particular, the connections between what they learn in class, and what they see in their family, community, state, or nation, can come as a surprise. In a lot of ways, social sciences and history are ideal components of an early college or dual enrollment curriculum, as they can hook students into subjects that they might not have thought of as relevant in high school, and might never have encountered in college given their trajectory. This is one of the powerful impacts dual enrollment or early college can have on students that people do not always predict – taking a college class at a specific point in high school can completely alter the students' academic trajectory. These high school years offer a real opportunity, as students are open to ideas about what they want to study or careers they want to pursue that may not be true either earlier or later in their academic careers.

Psychology is a subject that some students dive into in high school, but more often in college. As an early college/dual enrollment offering, psychology taught at the college level can be a powerful experience. For students in our program in Lawrence, Massachusetts, college-level psychology classes have been nothing short of a revelation. Students have told us that in their own family, mental illness is regarded as "faking," and not taken at all seriously as physical illness. In a college-level psychology class, learning about the brain, and the illnesses that can affect it, can open students' eyes to a different perspective on their families and communities. Psychology has been so popular that many students who have taken our engineering path sequence also take psychology, as they have heard so many positive things about it through their peers.

Lead to Launch: Isabelle Cherney, Ph.D.

Isabelle Cherney is a psychologist and Vice Provost at Merrimack College, where she has worked with the early college from the beginning. Her lessons are:

- Build a diverse team to work with your students, in order to better understand and support them.
- Offer students classes that let them understand more about themselves and their place in the world.
- Work with faculty so that they can better understand the students and their backgrounds.

Why Psychology Resonates with Early College Students

In our early college program at Merrimack College, one of the big surprises was how much our Lawrence students loved psychology as a field of study. School of Education and Social Policy Dean Isabelle Cherney Isabelle Cherney was promoted to Vice Provost, as her academic career has been spent in psychology, teaching it at both the graduate and undergraduate levels. She told me "Psychology is all about the human condition: the individual within a group, and trying to identify your own identity, the crucial development about individual worth and purpose." For high school students, "it's a great way for them to better understand who they are, why they do things, why society is pressuring them." For adolescents, who are obsessed with issues of their own identity, psychology provides a way of examining these issues in relation to society, as opposed to sociology, which is much more focused on systems than individuals.

Psychology also allows students to explore these issues in a scientific way. Much of introductory psychology addresses the brain, and to help them understand what their body and mind are doing, and how they are changing. Cherney told me,

> It also gives them a vocabulary to talk about what they are experiencing, both as individuals and in their family and school. It is an opportunity to gain self-confidence, and to have a better understanding of the social barriers that they are up against every day. Social sciences, drawing on data, also help give young people tools in their classes and beyond. They are better able to understand data and its uses, and be able to be more critical of it in the media.

Cherney points to motivation and engagement as reasons why early college students are so successful on the college campus. She says that they have *elan*, a power that they bring to the classroom, that is extraordinary for the faculty they teach.

> Early college students are in the process of unleashing the potential that they have, and faculty can literally feel the difference in the classroom. A good program is able to channel that energy, and is able to use it to build up students' self-efficacy and self-confidence.

According to Cherney, the key to a successful early college is to build a diverse team of individuals who can help understand the cultural, social and financial context of the students. This way, when faculty are struggling with how to deal with students or student issues, there is a rich array of perspectives to help everyone understand the place that the students are coming from.

Changes to Help Students Reach College Level Work

John Lovett had taught survey classes at the college level before taking on an early college political science course. However, he found that his traditional mix of papers and midterm/final was not helping his early college students at all. With fewer grades to go on than in their high school courses (where there might be multiple assignments for a grade each week), students were not doing well in his class, and did not know they were not reading and studying at the depth needed. Lovett changed the assessments in his class – he added another test, and changed the two papers for the class to focus more on connections to the present. He implemented these changes in both his early college and his freshman level college classes, and students generally did better with more opportunities to be assessed.

As a result of these changes, Lovett saw students connect more to the subject as well as to him as an instructor. He held his office hours for the class at the high school, and students began to stop by to talk about the class, and gradually, to talk about politics and life more generally. After the election in 2016, students who had been in the class the previous year stopped by as well to talk about the election and its implications. Through building stronger ties, Lovett ended up talking to students more about their college choices and writing letters of recommendation for them. These are exactly the kinds of relationships that education researcher Anthony Jack says that minority and low-income students need to make in the college context – personal connections with faculty members that can result in expanded opportunities and ideas about potential education and careers.

> ### 🗣 Real Teacher: Amber Hancock Bishop
>
> Amber Hancock Bishop has worked as a teacher at Early College Alliance @ Eastern Michigan University since the program started. Her lessons for teaching social science include:
>
> - Focus on the "soft skills" that students need to navigate college classes.
> - Do not neglect key skills such as reading, which students may have not mastered before enrolling in the early college program.
> - Teach social sciences in a thematic way – tackle big topics and big questions, rather than names or dates.

Teaching History, Social Studies, Soft Skills, and Reading in an Early College Program

Amber Hancock Bishop has a unique background as a teacher of history and social studies at ECA@EMU. She trained as a middle/high school social studies teacher, then worked as a tutor for a GEAR UP college access program, then was poached to become the founding history teacher in the early college. This combination of working with students where they are while keeping an eye on where they will be in the future defines her teaching and her career. In the midst of her work at ECA, she enrolled in graduate school and earned a master's in education in reading which has informed her work with 9th and 10th grade students who are on their way to college-level work, but need to build academic skills in reading and writing to get there.

To prepare students for early college experiences, Bishop focuses on the less glamorous parts of social science and history. She starts students out with the "soft skills" that students need to be able to navigate a college classroom. She works with students on how to read and take notes using a college-level history textbook. For students who are at risk of not moving on to college-level work, she teaches a class that focuses on vocabulary and reading strategies. Focusing on key words that students will see at the college level, she works with students on identifying vocabulary and using it in context. Without this instruction, students can find themselves skipping over key pieces of vocabulary, and in college-level readings, means that students can get through a reading passage without getting anything out of it.

Bishop's students also learn history through truly innovative pedagogy. She has taught world history classes using the Big History curriculum, taking students from the Big Bang to the present. Through integration of history and science, this curriculum gives students a chance to learn about the framework of world history, which will come in handy in any future history classes. Students also complete research projects on the Holocaust, researching a participant and tracing their journey through World War II. She has seen her students flourish with these strategies, and able to move on to college coursework prepared to tackle the challenges ahead.

Building Skills: Debates and Policy Papers

When Kirstie Dobbs appeared in my office for a job interview to teach political science for our program, it was not really an interview. I had only one goal – convince her to take the position working half of the time with our early college program, and the other half with traditional college students. She later told me that she almost did not apply for the position, as it seemed totally outside her experience and skill set. Though she was a researcher who specialized in youth political movements in Tunisia, she had no background or interest in being a traditional high school teacher, and almost ignored the job advertisement.

At first, she found the early college students different than those she had previously taught. They were less mature in a lot of ways, even giggly at times. She found that she had to tell them "time to focus." Over that first term, she learned that she had to set the expectation for seriousness. She also connected their joking behavior with a lack of confidence about college. She noted that "they start out not as confident, but all of that changes a few weeks into the class. They begin to figure out that this subject is approachable." In addition, Dobbs said, "I sometimes forget they are 16 years old, relatively sheltered, and sometimes they need more explaining about key concepts."

However, while the early college students were less mature than her traditional age students, Dobbs found them much more mature and self-reliant when it came to managing their lives and problems. Dobbs said,

> they are a lot more mature in terms of solving their own problems, such as in the COVID-19 situation, than my traditional students. The Early college students were more able to figure out all their internet access issues, and they are able to solve problems for themselves, when then the issues are outside their control.

She concluded, "When things got tough, early college students rose to the situation."

Students in the class come into the early college program already politically aware. Dobbs said,

> I am teaching at this point in time – their generation – Generation Z – is super diverse, way more educated, and a lot more politically mobilized than the previous generation. The students in Lawrence already feel anti-Trump, who explicitly called out the City of Lawrence as a source of drugs and crime. So when I am teaching them in an introductory political science class, they have the passion and energy, and are ready to go, but they need support, resources, and structure.

Dobbs has them write a policy paper as part of the early college class. She told me, "Their topics, such as the school to prison pipeline, take complex issues, and the students suggest the best ways to make change."

Dobbs said,

> When I am teaching the early college students, I know that my positionality is not at all similar to theirs and I acknowledge that. I don't know what this is like to be in their shoes. The best example of this is when we talk about immigration, we are facing serious issues and the professor does not have the answers for you, or the experience to connect with you.

This means that for Dobbs, she cannot just step into the classroom and pretend that she, as the professor, can just give students the answers to the big issues. The students need to have "ownership of their own knowledge, and make up their own mind about these issues."

Activities that Engage Early College Students in Politics and Civics

Early college students in Dobbs's class loved to debate, and Dobbs structured this activity so that students would need to research a topic and a side of a debate that is chosen randomly, so that they might not be arguing their own personal position on an issue. With issues that are politically "hot," this can cause high school students to resist, as they may need to argue the opposite side of an issue like abortion or immigration that they have strong feelings about. Researching and analyzing both sides of an issue, in order to develop an argument, is a powerful strategy for intellectual development, even as it means that students can suffer personal and intellectual discomfort in the process.

Dobbs also arranged the schedule so that Merrimack traditional students (overwhelmingly white and suburban) came and worked with the early college students on the debate activity. As a result, the early college students gained confidence, getting to see that their own work was on a par with their peers who were a few years older and already enrolled full time in college. The students further sharpened their skills with a policy paper that made an argument about an issue and potential changes. Some of the papers Dobbs received were so good that she is looking at getting them published, and found them comparable to graduate master's level papers.

To cover the material that an introduction to government class needs to include (three branches of government, etc.), Dobbs uses a flipped classroom model, in which students do the reading in advance and take a short online quiz. The students can have more than one attempt, and students overall have scored very well on theses (higher than their Merrimack peers). This has freed up time that Dobbs would have spent lecturing (which she did not find effective with these students), and instead allowed her to focus on discussions and activities during class time.

> ✅ **The Early College/Dual Enrollment Edge: Debates and Disagreements**
>
> Early college students get a lot out of debates. Here is what some of the research tells us:
>
> - Students learn a great deal from having to research one side of a debate, especially when they need to research a position they do not believe in.
> - Students struggle with how to decide between two positions that both seem "true," but this struggle helps them make advances in their own thinking.
> - Students, ultimately, learn that evidence is important in formulating a position, and that just having an opinion is not proof that one is correct.

William Perry's Scheme and Early College Students

Harvard professor William Perry was a major researcher of college students' learning in the 1960s and 1970s, and devised a "scheme" to understand the progression college students go through as they journey from freshman to senior year to adulthood (Perry, 1999).

- Students begin in dualism, in which everything has a true or false answer, and in which the professor or teacher is delivering the truth to students. The key to student success is to copy down the right answer in lectures, to memorize it, and to give it back on the test.
- Students then proceed to multiplicity, in which students realize that every opinion has merits, and that there is no certain way to decide which are true. The teacher, therefore, becomes less important, as she/he is only one person, whose opinion is no better than that of students. As a result, school is a challenge of figuring out the teacher or professors' game, and playing that game correctly.
- Finally, there are forms of relativism, in which students grasp that different opinions are backed by argumentation and evidence, and that

some answers may be more correct than others. Teachers become a partner in this discussion that seeks the truth, and ultimately, learning is making a commitment to an answer, even while knowing it has its limits.

Through early college social science coursework, students can engage in issues beyond those which their traditional high school curriculum provides. While many students in early college classes have also taken or will take AP classes, these do not provide the means to move up Perry's scheme. Instead, AP classes tend to become a vast information processing task, with students struggling to remember details for a myriad of historical periods or social science cases.

What early college social science classes can do is to provide students with activities such as debates and research papers that force students to contend with clashing opinions on issues that have no "right" answer. When asked to analyze an argument, particularly one which the student does not agree with, they are forced to rethink their own opinion, as well as their ideas about who might hold the opposing opinion. In Kirstie Dobbs's introduction to government class, students are assigned a side on a debate (such as immigration), and need to work with their group on presenting their strongest argument, and countering those of their opposition. Students also need to write a policy analysis on a topic of interest to them, in order to make a case for their own chosen proposal.

This forces students to move beyond their own opinion, to begin to understand those of others, and to make their own arguments based on evidence, not just opinion. These strategies, while they may frustrate students at the time, have a powerful impact. While providing support (Merrimack upper-class undergraduates help students with the paper, as does Dr. Dobbs), the class forces students to think about issues in a way that they might have only done in upper level courses in college.

Resource Toolbox

Perry Jr, W. G. (1999). *Forms of Intellectual and Ethical Development in the College Years: A Scheme.* Jossey-Bass Higher and Adult Education Series. Jossey-Bass Publishers, 350 Sansome St., San Francisco, CA 94104.

SECTION Three

The Broader Impact of Early College and Dual Enrollment Programs

How Early College and Dual Enrollment Programs Can Make a Difference for the Broader Community

Student Perspectives on the Dream of College

At the auditorium of Lawrence High School, in Lawrence, MA, the finalists for the sophomore class speech contest at Abbott Lawrence Academy were making their orations to a panel of judges that included the mayor of their city. Their city, Lawrence, Massachusetts, is among the poorest in the state of Massachusetts, and their city has a far smaller number of college graduates than the state average. But now, as part of a redesigned high school model, students throughout this building have an impressive range of options for their post-graduation plans, including early college options at Northern Essex Community College and Merrimack College.

However, despite these academic strengths and opportunities, students in speech after speech talked about the high cost of college, and the difficulties caused by student loans. Students questioned whether college was worth it, compared to the way their parents had moved ahead – not through higher education, but through employment (often more than one job, or a small business) and sheer hard work. Affordability and return on investment trumped all other issues for their students – their decision to attend college was based on a cost/benefit analysis, and college did not seem to be more attractive than work after high school.

For today's students who are growing up in urban areas, even those within minutes of a college campus, higher education is increasingly seen as out of reach financially, and as a poor investment of time and money.

This focus on affordability is why dual enrollment and early college options are vital for colleges and universities in urban areas serving low-income students. Early college and dual enrollment programs are underrated as a strategy for attracting talented low-income students, and as a means of helping students and families see a viable and affordable pathway to college.

> **Lead to Launch: Dr. Carlos Santiago, Commissioner, Massachusetts Department of Higher Education**
>
> Dr. Carlos Santiago has been leading the early college efforts in Massachusetts from the top, as Commissioner of the Department of Higher Education. In this role, he has learned:
>
> 1. If a program is called an early college, it needs to have partnership and collaboration between the higher education and K-12 partners.
> 2. Students in an early college are learning skills and information they need to navigate the college classroom and campus, not just content knowledge or academic skills.
> 3. This knowledge of the campus and the classroom can become a resource for families and communities across the state, not just for the students.

Dr. Carlos Santiago had many reasons to launch an early college strategy as the Commissioner of Massachusetts Department of Higher Education (DHE). He has been urged to take on this opportunity by two of his board members, Chris Gabrielle and Dr. Nancy Hoffman, and early college also fit as part of the DHE new "equity agenda." Santiago was disturbed by the lack of college success among students of color, even those from middle-income families. Research has found that in public college in Massachusetts, race was a more important predictor of graduation than class, and that even students of color from middle-income backgrounds finished college at a lower rate than low-income white students. For a public system in the most educated state on American, this would not do.

According to Santiago, early college programs could serve not only to reduce costs, but also to give students the information they need to successfully navigate what might be an alien system for them and their families. Santiago said,

> While students might be academically prepared for college by their high school, they might not have the information they need to successfully navigate the college classroom and campus – understanding the college bureaucracy, understanding the importance of key tests and assessments, how to make progress towards graduation. This information, specific to the college experience, gives early college students an edge, and helps reduce the gaps that the system has in graduation rates by race/ethnicity and class.

This spread of information can have a broader impact, according to Santiago, as it can then move from the student out through their peer, family, and community networks. As more students in areas such as gateway cities have the information to navigate college successfully, and feel confident about this, the college going and graduation rates will rise, providing new human capital resources for these areas.

Student Perspectives on Early College

When students in early college programs talk about their experiences, they point to both an individual gain of educational skills, but also to a broader community and civic impact that the program can have. Participating in an early college program, for students in cities such as Lawrence, is an act of resistance and defiance to the stereotypes about their city and about their community. Thus, early college programs are a way in which local colleges and universities can both support youth and the urban communities they are part of, and help redefine the public image of those communities. As one of early college students wrote about the Lawrence program:

> As a student in the Lawrence Public School system, it is easy to feel counted out. There are so many stereotypes of us being lazy, stupid, ungrateful, or uninterested. But in Abbott, everyone who is enrolled in these Merrimack courses has a goal, has big plans for their future. Allowing us to take these courses further prepares us for these bright futures we aspire to, and shows Lawrence in a different light. We aren't dropouts, class skippers, etc. A focal point of being an Abbott student is "being the future of Lawrence."

> This partnership with Merrimack College is helping not only us see that, but the rest of our city, and those around us ... Taking college classes has raised my self-esteem, and made me feel as though I am paving the way for my future.
>
> (Quoted in Cherney, et al., 2020)

Another Lawrence student, who was awarded a scholarship, connected the early college program to larger issues of community development and university/community relations in her graduation speech, stating:

> [The early college program] shows that Lawrence has so much to offer and that we are not "the city of the damned" as we have been portrayed as. ... This partnership between Abbott and Merrimack College is the first of its kind: kids are graduating high-school with college credits from a private 4-year university, and that is something to celebrate. Merrimack College is doing what other colleges or universities wish they could do: creating and maintaining hard-working and goal-oriented individuals who will stop at nothing to achieve their goals.

While students recognize the individual benefit to them as early college students, they are also keenly aware that the program has a wider benefit than just for themselves. Early college students often view the issue of affordability as one for the entire family, taking into account the issues for their siblings and their parents. Any savings that they can make as a student can free up funds for other purposes within the family, and avoid becoming a burden to other family members.

Students also recognize that through early college programs they can become role models and guides to their younger relatives and other community members. They will be praised for their achievement, but also expect to be asked to help out back at their high school or in their community. Finally, their work in the early college is political to students, and they point to it to refute what politicians and people in their region say about them. Students' success in early college can be used as proof that they, their families, and their community can make a contribution to their city, state, and nation.

Faculty Perspectives on Early College

"They are the type of students that college professors dream of teaching"

Despite the strong evidence about early college's effectiveness, if you ask college faculty, you will find widespread skepticism about these programs. Research in the Texas university system showed that, despite overwhelming positive evidence of early college success and achievement, faculty resisted the blurring of any lines between high school and college, and did not believe that students who completed early college coursework were ready to proceed to the next college class in the sequence. Overall, college faculty report a far less positive view of early college than high school teachers, perhaps because for many college faculty, teaching high school students is viewed as a step down in prestige, while for high school teachers, association with higher education can be viewed as a step "up."

However, faculty who have taught in early college programs report very positive results, both in terms of student engagement, and in terms of personal satisfaction. When asked, faculty members who have taught early college students report that this teaching is among the high points of their day, and that these students often bring a determination that they wish they saw more of in their traditional age undergraduates. One faculty member who teaches early college students said,

> These students are motivated, inquisitive, and thoughtful. One thing I really appreciate about them is that they have taken their education into their own hands. They are pursuing advanced work, they care about what they are doing, and it is truly helping them to get a head-start for their future.

Another early college faculty member viewed the long-term impact of the program as the most positive:

> The early college program not only helps students get into college, who might otherwise be marginalized from obtaining a college level degree, but ensures they have the necessary skill set to be successful throughout their college

career ... The early college program changes the lives of hard working, high achieving students, who possess an immense amount of drive to be positive change-makers in their communities.

The individual and group characteristics of the students in the program also stood out to faculty members. One wrote,

> These students are intelligent, curious, diligent, and especially driven. The early college students have demonstrated a maturity about their education that is rare and incredibly valuable. They always came to class prepared, and bursting with interesting questions, thought provoking stories, and encouragement for fellow classmates. Their drive to succeed was palpable. Their desire to learn was tangible. And their enthusiasm and energy in class made teaching so wonderfully fun.

During the pandemic of 2020, students in the early college program stood out as able to navigate the changes in instruction from in person to online. One faculty member said,

> The number one thing these particular students possess is grit. There are certain "valleys" in the semester when I can predict students to be tired and disenchanted, but not with my early college students. When other students feel like calling it quits, my early college students dig in, work hard, and persevere in ways that are truly admirable. As a cohort, they are the type of students that college professors dream of teaching because of their passion for learning and unwavering commitment to their education. This is why these students were also particularly well equipped to handle the school closures during the pandemic.

Another faculty member noted that the early college students change in their attitudes towards college, changes visible within even the single term that faculty work with them. One faculty member said,

> I notice in my students an increased sense of confidence and readiness as they move through the semester and one step closer to college and to adulthood. So many of us believe as teenagers that "we can't" or "we shouldn't," especially when it comes to expressing our thoughts, dreams and goals and what I see in my Early College students is an increased and developing sense that, in fact, they can and they should. That, in my opinion, is an immeasurable gift that Early College provides.

Finally, one of my colleagues ranks teaching for the early college among her peak experiences of her career. She said of the early college students,

> I have been teaching at the college level for a long time now and the experience of working with my Early College students is unlike any I have ever had. In addition to a classroom full of obviously smart people I am continuously bowled over by who my students are. Bringing with them an incredible blend of curiosity, tenacity, grit and energy, these students do more than rise to the challenges I present to them ... they challenge me to be at my best. Their fantastic abilities to wonder out loud, to want more than the facts and theories in the textbook and to agree and disagree with civility and respect are a much-needed breath of fresh air and inspiring. At the risk of sounding cliché, they are truly an inspiration, a total joy to know and I am honored to work with them.

The Early College/Dual Enrollment Edge:

The American Institutes of Research has studied the economic impact of early college, and found the following:

- The cost of early college programs is, on average, about $3,800.
- The average benefit is over $57,000.
- The ratio of benefit to cost of early college is over 15 to 1, meaning that each dollar invested in early college yields over 15 times its value for its beneficiaries and for the public.

The Impact on the Greater Community

What do members of the community get out of early college programs and experiences? While Americans have become accustomed to seeing education as a private good, purchased by individuals and families to get ahead, education is really part of a common effort for community development. Areas such as Lawrence are starved for college graduates. The lack of workers credentialed with associates or bachelors level degrees means that most members of the community are on a treadmill, working at jobs that do not pay enough to get ahead, and also lack long-term security from unemployment.

The lack of people in the community with college experience also leads to fewer adults available to help young people navigate their way to college.

In any community, parents, aunts, uncles, older brothers and sisters, pastors and priests are all needed to help young people make this jump to college successfully, and without a critical mass of these people, the young people are at a disadvantage.

When young people do not attend college, employers lose out too. Lawrence was once home to enormous mills that provided generations of immigrants with jobs making shoes and textiles. While manufacturing is still vibrant in the Merrimack Valley, it is a smaller piece of the employment picture, and many of the jobs in these enterprises require college or advanced technical training for employment. Even enterprises that welcome high school graduates as entry level employees encourage further education once in the workforce to advance.

Lack of college degrees affects the community as a whole. With college education and higher earnings come greater spending at local businesses, higher homeownership rates, better overall health and wellness, and higher civic engagement. Communities without options for higher education have suffered greatly during and after the recession of 2008, hit hard by unemployment, and slow to rebuild after. (For overall impact of higher education on communities, see Rothwell, 2015.)

💡 Lead to Launch: Odanis Hernandez

Based on her experience with Work-Based Education and Lawrence High School's Early College Program, Ms. Hernandez suggests that new programs:

- Build and empower a staff to run the college/dual enrollment program.
- Recruit an early college/dual enrollment team that is culturally sensitive and aware.
- Make family engagement proactive and intentional.

How Community Partners can Help Early College and Dual Enrollment Programs

Community partners can help in many ways. Direct funding of efforts is ideal, but help in arranging internships and job shadowing opportunities is also a welcome way to build motivation for students in the program. Partners can provide needed publicity, such as highlighting the program, or helping produce high-quality videos, to get the story of the early college options out to the community. The Eastern Leaders group, a public-private partnership in Michigan, produced a series of videos featuring students involved in different secondary options, which helped build support, enrollment, and excitement for these programs.

While the "buzz" that business and others can create is important for enrollment, in the long term, the community needs to insist on higher expectations. Early college founder Dave Dugger told me: "In the start-up phase it is critical to create both a buzz and an expectation of 'what is possible'." However, Dugger wants these partners to also become more demanding on the system. He told me,

> Where I think the process can be improved is getting the business and government to become insistent on transformation of the current system, rather than supporting another program within the system – business and government entities should be insisting on every student having some college credits before high school graduation.

Early colleges are a bafflingly difficult sell in today's education policy marketplace. While they save taxpayer dollars, improve outcomes, and assist educational institutions, their beneficiaries often lack the political connections that have boosted other reform efforts. Place-based scholarships and free college programs tend to draw more local support. As an effort that exists between institutions, early colleges fall between the cracks of traditional educational policy in most states.

Resource Toolbox

American Institutes for Research. (2013). *Early College, Early Success: Early College High School Initiative Impact Study*. Washington, DC.

Atchison, D., Zeiser, K.L., Mohammed, S., Knight, D.S. and Levin, J. (2019). The Costs and Benefits of Early College High Schools. *Education Finance and Policy*, 1–56. doi: 10.1162/edfp_a_00310

Cherney, I., Douglas, L., Fischer, E. and Olwell, R. (2020). Early College High School/Dual Enrollment 2.0: Evidence-Based Approaches to

Engage Youth and Families for Educational, Career, and Community Development. *Metropolitan Universities, 31*(2), 18–32. doi: 10.18060/23815

Jobs for the Future, Early College. (2019). https://www.jff.org/what-we-do/impact-stories/early-college/. Retrieved November 14, 2020.

Rockwell, J. (2015). What Colleges Do for Local Economics: A Direct Measure Based on Local Spending. Brookings Institute Website. https://www.brookings.edu/research/what-colleges-do-for-local-economies-a-direct-measure-based-on-consumption/. Retrieved November 14, 2020.

Simon's Rock College, History. (2019). https://simons-rock.edu/early-college/understanding-early-college/our-history/history.php. Retrieved November 14, 2020.

Supporting Early College and Dual Enrollment Students' Health and Well-Being

Adjusting to College Life and Stress

Educators, parents, and community members cannot help but notice that students' struggle for well-being, physical and mental, is more visible. For folks in education for the last decade, the upsurge of students at the K-12 level or on campus who need help dealing with health issues is stunning, with student self-reports of health issues rising each year. At the college level, reports of anxiety and depression are common across campus, and are at the root of many academic problems.

Part of the struggle that college students face is a deeply unhealthy lifestyle. On their own for the first time, often with a lot less structure than high school, college freshmen tend to sleep poorly, eat substandard food, not take care of themselves physically, and struggle with any illness that might occur. In many cases, students were helped by the structure of high school, and rejected the things that helped keep them on track in the past when they arrived at college, often with terrible results.

Early college and dual enrollment programs can actually be part of the solution to some of these issues, as the students in these programs get to try out college work while they still have the day-to-day support of their parents, and access to the resources at their high school. They get a chance to learn how to manage a college schedule, and the increased time needed for study with the help of many more adults than most college students have in a traditional freshman year.

Maintaining Mental Health

Early college/dual enrollment students are simultaneously in two highly stressful settings – high school and college. High school students are under pressure academically and socially, and are at higher risk of depression and suicide. While society tends to romanticize the college experience, the reality can be very different – many students struggle with anxiety and depression, made worse by the idea that they should be experiencing the "best years of their lives." The age groups of high school and college students are also times that are the time of onset for many mental illnesses, such as depression and schizophrenia. (For problems among college students, see https://www.activeminds.org/about-mental-health/statistics/.)

Students struggle with the concept of mental health as well. For many families and communities, mental illness can be a taboo issue, or not recognized as a legitimate disorder. At a workshop on college interviewing, one of our early college students told us that what she was passionate about was mental health, as people in her family with mental illness were accused of "faking" an illness. While this is at an extreme, many people in high school and college settings still treat mental illness as far different than physical illness, often downplaying the impact of mental illness on school work and life without thinking through the impact of these illnesses. The National Association of Secondary School Principals has identified mental health as a key area for their schools to address, in order to improve academic achievement and student well-being (NASSP 2019).

Early college programs and programs that work with high school students need to think proactively about the mental health of students, and design stigma-free ways to address the issue. One high performing school I have worked with devised a short protocol to help students calm down when they feel overwhelmed, and posted it throughout the building. Other schools have devised ways of working mindfulness into the school day or after-school curriculum, using this as a setting where students dealing with mental illness, as well as those just dealing with stress or life, can come together to address these issues. Classical High School in Providence, RI, has a "midnight waffles" club to promote mental health through fun activities such as stand-up comedy, blowing bubbles, and re-doing the dialogue to videos.

Taking psychology classes as part of early college programming can bring a much-needed perspective for high school students. While some high schools offer AP psychology, most do not. Students in Merrimack's introduction to psychology early college class have been lively questioners and discussants in class, and several have indicated that they now intend to minor or major in the field in college. This is an example of how early colleges not only help students get ahead in their credits, but also have the potential to change their ideas, with impact both inside and outside the classroom.

On campuses, student-led efforts such as Active Minds have sought to de-stigmatize mental health issues, and to support students who might be wrestling with them (Active Minds, 2019). While these efforts encourage students to pursue therapy and help, they also focus on just helping students set goals and work towards them each day. Campuses struggle with the profusion of smartphones and social media, which both isolate students (even those living on campus) and provide a constant source of social comparison that can wear on students' sense of well-being.

Lead to Launch: Bryan Landgren

Bryan is a mental health advocate and has been a phone/text counselor with Samaritans, a suicide prevention organization. His advice for helping students address their mental health include:

- Try to understand the unique stress early college/dual enrollment students are living with.
- Give students more chances to try out activities and succeed, rather than assume that they can do things correctly the first time.
- Make it clear that it is always ok to ask for support, whether it is related to academics or to mental health.

Bryan Landgren brings significant background in mental health and wellness to his work with early college students – he has worked for Samaritans, a mental health support line, as well as doing research on the mental health needs of college students as part of his M.Ed. capstone project. He has developed workshops for early college students locally, as well as led national webinars in mental health and suicide prevention.

Landgren sees mental health and stress management as key components of early college programs. Landgren told me

> for early college students, junior year is a big stressor for them. They need to grow up and mature so quickly, and this induces anxiety in their brains. The hardest part for them is not having people who understand what they are going through. They are facing tough classes in both high school and college, but neither group of teachers or staff fully understands the level of stress students are under.

Then in senior year, the added pressures of the college admission process, and the sense that reaching out for help is a weakness, can degrade student mental health as well.

Due to the fact that early college students are selected for their program, they are also expected to do everything right the first time they see it. Recently, in a Blackboard training with early college students, Landgren realized that the assumption was that having seen Blackboard once, they were fully ready to use it in class – despite the fact that traditional age college students struggle with the system on a daily basis.

For students in early college programs, this stress, and the anxiety that results, just adds up. Landgren notes that

> As brain research has shown, their brains are not going to be fully developed until at least age 21 (if not 25). But students may be struggling with pressures at home, difficulty work at school, stress in the college classroom, all leading to anxiety.

Added to this, students do not always feel it is OK to ask for help, and can feel that they need to achieve perfect scores and straight As, even when this is an unrealistic goal.

Landgren feels that mental health needs to be built into early college programs from the beginning, and needs to form part of the curriculum as well. Rather than focusing early activities and orientation on academics and program logistics, Landgren believes early programming needs to include information on how students can navigate this process while maintaining mental wellness. In addition, classes such as psychology and human development in early college programs can give students information and a vocabulary to discuss how their brains work, and to encourage all students to seek help if they need it. Finally, as early college and dual enrollment opportunities are offered to a wider range of students, this can have a positive impact on student mental health, giving them a wider range of peers to interact with, and decreasing the sense of being in a pressure cooker.

Finding Time to be More than a Student

Part of the challenge of being a student in an intrinsically stressful environment, such as an early college, is finding ways to disconnect. The long college admissions process can make students feel as though they need to achieve in every part of life, using all available moments. School is important, as are test scores (and test prep), leadership activities, community service, political involvement, and now the addition of creating your own company or organization. These can add up to feelings of being overwhelmed, and lead even the highest achieving students to feelings of despair.

Early college students need time to be adolescents, as well as high achieving students. This can involve skateboarding, playing hacky-sack, laying around and reading a book, or otherwise enjoying time with or without peers. While these activities might appear to be loafing to well-meaning parents and adults, all human beings need some time that is not committed to achieving some sort of abstract goal, but is a chance for the brain to recharge.

Community service activities, particularly those that involve getting to know the people you serve, can also help level out students' thinking. Working in a soup kitchen where you eat with the people served can help young people connect to people they might not ordinarily meet, and will also give them a sense of making a contribution to their community. Our high school partner, Abbott Lawrence Academy, has a community service requirement, and hosts a day of service each fall, where students go out and volunteer at community agencies one day each December. Activities such as Best Buddies and Special Olympics–Young Athletes, can also take students out of their own heads, and ask them to make a connection with someone whose life is quite different from their own.

Physical activity and nutrition are another key to well-being for students at any level. This might take the form of a sport, or intramurals, or just going for a run or a walk. Many early college students take on individual sports rather than team sports, to fit with their schedule. Having a regular physical activity to do, and eating relatively healthy meals, can go a long way to keeping students from "crashing." Music, vocal or instrumental, can help students unplug from the stresses of daily life. Having some form of spiritual practice or meditation, such as prayer, meditation, organized religious services, or Mindfulness Based Stress Reduction, helps students process and deal with the stresses that they cannot avoid.

Connecting to Community Programs

Given their funding structures, early college programs should not try to "go it alone." The American educational system, for all its problems, has an amazing array of educational and community organizations that can step up and help students. In the Lawrence High School early college program, many organizations, such as Top-Notch Scholars, SquashBusters and YDO, provide a great deal of college-readiness/access programming to students. They are organizations that work with students starting in middle school, and have built relationships of trust with students and families even before high school, that they can draw on.

Think hard about the community resources you can draw on. Local health centers can provide programming and career mentoring; local companies can host job shadowing days; non-profit and volunteer organizations often have programming or scholarship programs that can help young people. Each connection you can make on behalf of your program could really help a student or family down the line, as you will not know the full needs of your program and participants for some time.

> ### ✓ The Early College/Dual Enrollment Edge: Dr. Michael Sayler
>
> Dr. Sayler has researched and worked with early college and dual enrollment students and programs as a researcher in gifted education. He suggests, based on research:
>
> 1. Take the social and emotional status of students seriously. If they are genuinely unhappy in their program, they will drop out, even if they are academically successful.
> 2. Make sure that students are appropriately challenged. If students are truly bored with the school curriculum, they will tune out or act out.

Dr. Michael Sayler's career has come full circle with early college and dual enrollment issues. He began his career writing a dissertation at Purdue on the experiences of students who enrolled in college full time before they turned 17, and the impact this experience had on them. He went on to work as a faculty member and as an administrator at the University of North Texas, which had a pioneering program that brought academically talented high school students to live on campus and take college classes in STEM areas. And he is currently Dean of Education at Eastern Michigan University on a campus with a lively early college program.

Sayler describes the early colleges at North Texas as unique, as students lived on campus, and were expected to pursue coursework that would lead to careers in science, engineering, or pre-health careers. At the time Sayler started his research on the program the focus was on the social-emotional well-being of the students – whether they were happy with the program, or missed their home high schools and their families. The TAMS program that Sayler researched became less diverse in many ways as time went on, as more affluent and motivated families found their way into the program, changing the mix of students.

Many students flourished in the program, with some finishing their TAMS career taking graduate level math classes at the university. However, some students did drop out of the program for academic or social-emotional reasons, and many dreaded returning to their home high school defeated – some did a GED program to avoid this shame, or attended another high school. Some students ran afoul of TAMS zero tolerance policy for drugs and alcohol (they lived together in one dorm on campus), a real temptation on a residential college campus.

As a researcher in gifted education, Sayler views early college as a real benefit for academically talented students. Without interventions such as early college, some students will become bored and disengaged in a traditional high school curriculum, and may even act out as a result. For students with this level of motivation, early college promises to truly engage these students, even when it means they may give up some of the normal social and even family life to pursue the opportunity

Resource Toolbox

Active Minds Website. https://www.activeminds.org/. Retrieved November 14, 2020.

Mayhew, M.J., Pascarella, E.T. and Terenzini, P.T. (2016). *How College Affects Students*. San Francisco, CA: Jossey-Bass.

National Association of Secondary School Principals. Position Statement: Mental Health. https://www.nassp.org/policy-advocacy-center/nassp-position-statements/promoting-mental-health-in-middle-level-and-high-schools/. Retrieved November 14, 2020.

Sayler, M.F. (2015). Texas Academy of Mathematics and Science: 25 Years of Early College STEM Opportunities. *Roeper Review, 37*(1), 29–38. doi: 10.1080/02783193.2015.975773

Outside the Early College/ Dual Enrollment Classroom
Extracurriculars, Sports, Clubs, and Work

The high school students are divided into two groups. One group, sitting in a colonial-era conference room on the campus of Phillips Academy – Andover, is working on homework with the assistance of a staff member. A participant brings in a FAFSA for help from the staff, a vast pile of financial documents entrusted by the parents to the program. The other group, deep in the bowels of an ancient gymnasium complex, are putting on their sneakers, getting out on the indoor courts, and most importantly, getting their squash balls warm enough to start playing. Lawrence program director Dora Lubin introduced me to the organization's approach, and it has benefited many students in Boston, Lawrence, Providence, and beyond.

This is SquashBusters, which starts working with students in 6th grade, and continues support into their college years. The program supports students with academics, physical activity, and building a supportive cohort of students, overseen by a professional staff trained in positive youth development. This means that their concern is always with the whole student and the whole family, and eventual success in life; not with producing professional athletes. When it comes to combining sports, academics, parental support, college access, and long-term support onto the college campus, SquashBusters is at the top of the game. The organization also manages to bring support from the wider squash community to these students, and to literally build structures on campuses that embody the program's aspirations.

> **Lead to Launch: Robert Snowden, Ph.D.**
>
> Dean Robert Snowden has created an early college/dual enrollment program in his work at Los Rios Community College District. He has worked to develop ways of recruiting young people who otherwise might not identify themselves as college material through their out of class interests:
>
> - Snowden started his program through teaching high school students communications – television and radio production. This attracted a diverse and motivated group of students who hungered to have access to the community college's equipment.
>
> - Snowden is able to leverage what students are interested in outside the classroom to bring them deeper into the college curriculum. He used student interest in creating media projects to convince them to try more academic media studies classes. He is building new certificate programs to draw students to the college, including one in Social Justice, tapping into student interest.
>
> - Snowden reviews all admissions files for his early college and advanced education (dual enrollment) program to find students who may, on paper, not have the GPA needed, but who will thrive in the new environment.

The Challenges of Sports and Extracurriculars for Early Colleges and Dual Enrollment Students

For everything that traditional comprehensive high schools do poorly (academics, engagement, equity), they excel at delivering sports, extracurricular, and social activities. Even at high schools where the graduate rate is modest, and the dropout rate is high, students moving through the system have a variety of options to feel included in the school, and to contribute to school spirit. This can be taken to the point where it is dysfunctional – where a school district, in danger of being closed down for poor performance by the state, assigned its administrators to help build floats for a homecoming parade.

Many early colleges have moved in the other direction completely. Some early college programs either have no sports or extracurriculars on their own, or they simply allow students to participate in their activities at their local schools. Many early college programs encourage students to participate in more individual sports (think fencing or running) than team activities. Many of the families attracted to early college, immigrant families in particular, are not seeking a high-powered sports program from their school, leading to less demand for investment in this area.

For students in dual enrollment classes, sports may or may not interfere with classes. For many programs, a college class might take place at high school after-school hours, prime time for sports. College courses also have more out of time studying and preparation, making them difficult to fit into a schedule of practices, workouts, and games. While some students are able to balance all these activities (much as they will have to as college athletes), many students let some responsibilities drop in the process.

Having sports and athletics as a less important part of high school allows early colleges far more flexibility in organization and staffing. Athletics shapes the structure of American education in a myriad of ways, not always productive. The need for late afternoon practice times means that high schools often begin before dawn in the winter. Without a football or basketball program, early college programs can start at 9 am instead. Schools that do not need to hire teachers in dual teacher/coach roles have much more flexibility in staffing. Without athletics and athletic events on their agendas, administrators have more time to focus on students and instruction.

While sports can build leadership and teamwork skills, schools with a less developed sports program channel that energy into other areas – one high performing International Baccalaureate high school has a debate program that rivals the size of a football team. Students learn leadership, teamwork, and service in many ways, and early colleges can tap into these, though this is countercultural.

The biggest point of resistance for students and families can be the pursuit of a college athletic career. While colleges and coaches have ably marketed the college athletic scholarship as a way to pay for college, the free-ride athletic scholarship is an elusive item in American higher education. Given the number of students participating in high school sports, the chances of playing sports at a college level, or of competing for a team offering scholarships, is low. The NCAA's own data on this issue is revealing: of 27 sports tracked, in only five sports are students more than 10%

likely to go on to play in college sports (NCAA, 2018). In the most lucrative sports, men's basketball and football, the percentages of high school athletes moving on to any college team are 4% and 7%, respectively. So great is the student and family investment in the idea of a college sports career, that colleges can offer students a lower scholarship labeled as an athletic scholarship than they would have had to offer as merit aid or a tuition discount.

What sports do provide, and that can also be provided in other ways, is some much-needed physical activity for young people. Some schools have looked to other methods of doing this, such as offering activities such as yoga during the school day as an elective. Early college graduate Paul Akande got all his exercise through a school ultimate frisbee team, which filled the hole left by the lack of a big sports program quite nicely. Sports also provide a sense of community and school pride, and early colleges have implemented activities to mirror the sense of excitement that sports can bring to a school.

How Out-of-School Activities Can Help Students

Extracurricular activities are a tricky issue for early college and dual enrollment students. As minors on a college campus, sometimes a residential college campus, early college students fall in between the worlds of high school and college activities. Many college activities resist the idea of having high school students involved, as the legal and other issues involved in working with minors are beyond what most college instructors and staff want to address. The presence on college campuses of dorms also makes early college students a group that needs to be watched over, given the ease with which conversation in class, a dining hall, or dorm can lead to students heading over to a residential space (Mayhew, M. J., Pascarella, E. T., & Terenzini, P. T. 2016).

However, early college students also derive a great deal of meaning from being part of a campus, and the flurry of activities that can take place. When racist graffiti was found on the campus of Eastern Michigan University, early college students attended protest marches, and even organized their own events to show their support of diversity and inclusion on campus.

Early college programs can also organize their own clubs and activities. Some of these can be very simple – ECA@EMU's first clubs included a book club that met every week after school to talk about what they were reading.

Sarah Cowdell, director of the Merrimack College Pioneer Scholars program found that her early college alumni were not always interested in connecting to activities on campus. While they had participated in a wide variety of sports and afterschool activities in high school, once on a college campus full time, many did not seek out clubs or activities. Instead, they prioritized classwork, then off-campus jobs, and put off the idea of joining activities or clubs, even those that were job related, until future semesters. Getting students to see the connections in campus engagement, especially those that will help build a career network, is a key task for anyone working with early college students.

The Question of Work

For most educators, students holding down a part-time job during high school or an early college program is not considered ideal. The conventional thinking in schools and colleges is that if students just devoted all of their time to school, they would have more time on task, and be more academically successful. While this is certainly true after a number of hours of work (20 plus per week), research has shown that many high school and college students make gains from having a job, and are able to balance their responsibilities quite well. They also report that they learn important skills on the job, make social connections, and gain self-esteem from earning a wage and contributing to their family.

When early college students are working part-time, program staff can encourage them to make connections between the learning they are making in the classroom, their current job, and what they might want to do next in college or in their career. If students can feel engaged about both work and school, they can build time-management and other skills that will carry them into college, where they will have the same issues to balance.

Some researchers, such as Jobs for the Future's (JFF) Dr. Nancy Hoffman, have gone further, suggesting that more work-based experiences be built into educational programs, and that coursework deals explicitly with issues of the workplace. While high income students are easily connected through their social networks to internships and opportunities, low-income students are often shut out of these, left to scrounge in their neighborhoods for entry level opportunities. Through programs that explicitly connect students to workplaces, and provide training in building and using social capital through networking, early college students could get a better chance of getting the types of positions that could help them advance their career aspirations (Hoffman, 2015).

Models to Provide Well-Rounded Early College Experiences

Research has shown that co-curricular activities in college can greatly strengthen the experiences that students have in and outside the classroom. The leadership, teamwork and service skills that are developed in these activities can have a long-term positive impact on students. The level of engagement students can feel, and the amount of good they can do for the community, can be impressive. The same arguments apply to early college students. Developed slowly and intentionally, activities outside the classroom can support and enhance the experience a great deal. As colleges struggle with getting their traditional undergraduates off their phones and out of their dorm rooms, we have an opportunity to give early college students an early start on becoming a positive and engaged part of campus.

Many of the early college students continue to get a great deal out of participating in the activities of their large high school as well. The early college students took on major roles in the school's production of Aida, in spite of their busy academic schedules. However, for the early college students, extracurriculars are not an overwhelming focus on their lives, which remains fixed on academics.

Outside the Classroom

Lead to Launch: Ellen Fischer

Dr. Ellen Fischer has worked for years to build student engagement as the principal of Early College Alliance in Ypsilanti, Michigan. Her lessons about student engagement include:

1. Student engagement builds over time. It might start with clubs and activities and build to bigger issues.
2. Early college students need a chance to address issues in their life and on campus.
3. Students can become leaders in this process, and to run their own events and discussions about engagement.

According to Ellen Fischer, early college students do participate in Eastern Michigan University clubs and activities – musical theater, orchestra, band, marching band, language clubs (we've had several officers in these), biology, physics, economics clubs, and even intramural sports (dodge ball and football). They also take part in extracurriculars in their districts, and many of them do that – sports, musicals, and some clubs like Robotics.

ECA also built an active student leaders group, of 50+ students, who do everything from serving as Ambassadors (they present at Information Nights, Shadow Days, and any time we have visitors) to producing events (Prom, Talent Show, Harvest Hangout). The students have a service component for their events, like a small fundraiser or "drive" of some sort. One of the subcommittees of student leaders is the Diversiteam – which also includes younger students who attend the Diversity Forum in our county and then become diversity educators with the other students.

Students also have a Memorial Garden outside of King Hall, planted in honor of two students who died during the school year. At the end of the first term ECA students have a CLICK Celebration & Luncheon, which celebrates surviving the first semester at ECA, as well as a Salute to Spring event (run by student leaders) at the end of the Winter term. The students have orientation events for incoming students in the summer, and a Back to School

Kickoff for Returning Students. ECA is considering adding a Graduation for completing students, but so far have had a dinner and celebration for our Completers.

> ## ✓ The Early College/Dual Enrollment Edge: Early College and Dual Enrollment Students Outside the Classroom
>
> Early college and dual enrollment students report:
>
> 1. They enjoy the diversity of the college setting, which is often far greater than their high school.
> 2. They enjoy fitting in with older students, and appreciate their maturity and seriousness.
> 3. They get academic support from their peers in study groups, and these often evolve into friendship.

What Early College Students Gain Outside the Classroom

Researchers Denise McDonald and Tina Farrell (2012) conducted focus groups with early college students to ask them about their own experiences, and how this fit into their future trajectory (high school to college to career). What they learned is that early college students, while stressed about their course workload and their future career, gained a lot from the early college experience that was not just inside the classroom:

- Early college students appreciated being in a setting that was more diverse from their high school, as well as more welcoming and inclusive. They felt accepted in the program far more than in their traditional high school, where some described their position as being "outcast from the outcasts."

- Early college students enjoyed their interactions with traditional age and older college students, and the maturity they saw in their classrooms

motivated them to act more responsibly and inspired them to academically achieve. Being not recognized as a high school student was a mark of achievement for the early college students.
- Early college students built informal networks for studying and support, and found these relationships helped them achieve, thrive, and persist through tough times. They found their peers a key area of academic support, so long as they were not perceived as procrastinators or otherwise irresponsible by their peers.
- Early college students reported both positive peer pressure (to achieve in class) and the absence of some of the negative peer pressure in their high school, such as not acting smart or being identified as academically talented or hardworking. The early college set them free of the need to "sandbag" or to act stupid to gain peer approval.

Resource Toolbox

National College Athletics Association (2018). Estimated Probability of Competing in College Athletics. http://www.ncaa.org/about/resources/research/estimated-probability-competing-college-athletics. Retrieved November 14, 2020.

Hoffman, N. (2015). *Let's Get Real Deeper Learning and the Power of the Workplace*. Cambridge, MA: Jobs for the Future. https://www.luminafoundation.org/files/resources/lets-get-real.pdf   Retrieved November 15, 2020.

McDonald, D. and Farrell, T. (2012). Out of the Mouths of Babes: Early College High School Students' Transformational Learning Experiences. *Journal of Advanced Academics, 23*(3), 217–248. doi: 10.1177/1932202X12451440

Mayhew, M. J., Rockenbach, A. N., Bowman, N. A., Seifert, T. A., Wolniak, G. C. with Pascarella, E. T. and Terenzini, P. T. (2016). *How College Affects Students (Vol. 3): 21st Century Evidence That Higher Education Works*.

SECTION Four

Building Sustainable Programs

Measuring Impact to Build Sustainable Early College and Dual Enrollment Programs

This chapter covers two of the most critical issues for the long-term survival and success of early colleges: evaluating the impact of your program and finding the resources to sustain this work. These two areas are interrelated, because most funders now want to see evaluation data even before they consider funding an effort. Interestingly, early college funding has long trailed its evidence of effectiveness. An long list of high school reforms have received major infusions of federal funding. However, there has been limited investment in early college initiatives, which is surprising because of the large body of data that supports their effectiveness.

> **Lead to Launch: Lane Glenn, President, Northern Essex Community College, Massachusetts**
>
> Lane Glenn became involved in early college and dual enrollment in his time in Michigan, where he worked with two communities (Pontiac and Auburn Hills) to create programs for students not on track for college. His lessons on building programs include:
>
> 1. Community colleges need to build early college and dual enrollment programs for students who are on the fence about whether college is for them. These students are also more likely to be place-bound and will stay in the community after graduation.

2. Institutions need to set important and far-reaching goals. In Lawrence, Massachusetts, Northern Essex Community College is committed to raising the percentage of the population with a college degree by 100%, and hopes in the long-term to double that percentage again.
3. Leaders need to fundraise in their communities for early college and dual enrollment programs, as legislative priorities can change, and even promised funding can dry up after a few years.

Measuring Early College/Dual Enrollment Impact

For most early college programs, it can be quite straightforward to collect data on student performance. Many programs track the demographics of the students who are in the program; they separate out the subgroups of students in the program (English language learners, students receiving special education services, non-white students). They often examine the academic outcomes of the students in the program (grades and pass rates). This is often supplemented with surveys and focus groups of participants. A next step in evaluation would be to follow alumni into their higher education or workforce context and try to make a case for their long-term success as a reflection of the program's impact.

These are all key measures but are not considered strong evidence in the world of educational research. As early colleges draw motivated students, they can be seen as a cut above their peers. Unless early colleges can show that their students are roughly equivalent to other regular high school students, or can show that the program has randomized admissions, evidence of impact is vulnerable to criticism.

Rigorous research from the Massachusetts Departments of Elementary & Secondary Education and Higher Education demonstrates that early college programs have a positive relationship on college course taking, academic achievement, high school graduation rates, FAFSA completion, and college enrollment after high school. Using the state's K-12 data system, researchers took each early college student, and identified a "peer" somewhere else in the state to provide a fair comparison of the impact of these programs.

The results of this study were striking. Demographic analysis showed that the vast majority of students in early colleges in the state are students of color, and that most are economically disadvantaged as well. Relative to their matched peers, students in Massachusetts early college programs earned college credits at a rate far higher, and they also were much more likely to complete the FAFSA and to enroll in college.

Students in Lawrence, Massachusetts, literally led the state when it came to their outcomes. Nearly all (94%) of 12th graders were headed for college, most (77%) had completed their FAFSA, and the vast majority (85%) had earned 12 or more credits with a C or higher average. In each of these areas, Lawrence early college students far exceeded the achievement of the matched pair students by 20 or more percentage points.

These results occurred during an academic year (2019–20) in which students were stressed and often cut off from the supports that traditionally help them apply for colleges, complete financial aid forms, and avoid the summer melt that plagues low-income students who get accepted to college, but do not show up in September for their classes. High school students told us that early college motivated them to stay connected with their courses, with their college courses taking top priority.

✓ The Early College/Dual Enrollment Edge:

According to national research by the American Institutes of Research:

- Early colleges generate at least 15 times return on investment for every dollar put into programming.
- Early college graduates gain over $33,000 in direct benefit to themselves as a result of attending the program.
- The public gets an extra $24,000 in benefit from the student attending early college, in the form of increased taxes and reduced benefits that need to be spent.

Measuring Long-Term Success and Return on Investment

Researchers at the American Institutes of Research (AIR) have evaluated early colleges at the largest scale. AIR is a top non-profit organization that takes on national and state-level evaluation projects to better understand the impact of policy interventions such as early college. Like most top researchers in the field of early college and dual enrollment, Dr. Kristine Zeiser came from the field of demography and social policy, with an interest in inequality. She joined AIR in the middle of studies of early college impact, particularly those looking at the long-term impact of the intervention. Unlike most educational interventions, early colleges had the advantage of being at a scale where randomized studies were possible, and long-term longitudinal studies were also becoming more doable.

The key to the long-term study was the National Student Clearinghouse, which holds almost all of the data in the United States on where students attend college and the progress that they are making each year. Zeiser said, "I want to stick with early college students until they are 50." However, there is still not an easy way to connect early college students to both their educational record and then on to the employment and earnings data. This next step would allow researchers to more accurately capture the longitudinal impact of early college and investigate whether the head start that early college graduates get turns into long-term gains, or fades as the students get older and the more conventionally educated students catch up.

Zeiser noted that there were some preconceptions that she sees her research fighting against. One of the biases against early college and dual enrollment is the fact that so many programs are based in community colleges. As a result, many policymakers and members of the public associate the programs with getting two-year degrees, then stopping and heading into the labor market. However, Zeiser's research showed that students in early college, even if they were attending a community college-based program, were more likely to seek a four-year degree immediately upon graduation (75% headed to four-year institutions) and to complete their degrees.

Early college is, for researchers, a tough sell. Zeiser said that some in education still regard early college and dual enrollment as "fake college," even though the quantitative data shows the impact on students' lives. She argued that researchers need to get inside the early college classroom and do more qualitative research to help document what happens inside that classroom and how it compares to the standard college classroom.

AIR's Dr. Drew Atchison became involved in early college through his work in educational finance, and he became a leader in studies of returns on investment of early college. He found that students in these programs made tremendous gains, and that these gains were found in not only private benefits (to the student) but also public benefits (greater taxes paid, less unemployment). The AIR team's 2019 study found that "[Early-college] programs cost approximately $950 more per student per year than traditional high school programs, or $3,800 per student for the four years of high school. The benefits of [early college] resulting from the higher educational attainment of [early-college] students amount to slightly more than $57,000. The result is a net present value (NPV) of almost $54,000 and a benefit-to-cost ratio of 15.0." This is a striking finding, as most interventions deliver less return at a much higher cost.

The researchers from AIR believe that early college and dual enrollment programs have a significant role in higher education, to help traditionally underserved students to be better prepared academically for college and to identify the right post-secondary institutions in which to enroll. They also see early college as a way to support these students during the process, in a way that a traditional dual enrollment program does not.

Researching Early College and Dual Enrollment: Brian An

Dr. Brian An, a quantitative educational researcher at the University of Iowa, has been among the most influential people in the field of documenting the impact of dual enrollment and early college programs. His work has shaped state level policy, as well the general perception that researchers have about the field.

From the beginning of his research, An found that his fellow college faculty were the most skeptical about dual enrollment and early college programs, even when then quantitative evidence of their positive impact was strong. Faculty might object that Advanced Placement classes were better preparation than dual enrollment. Faculty also often focused on the college search and enrollment process in terms of selective colleges, which relatively few American students attend, while dual enrollment programs flourished in systems with public colleges that could offer coursework and accept the credits.

When An started in the field, there were relatively few researchers working on the issues of dual enrollment and how it impacted student achievement and affordability. That has changed, as An now gets at least a manuscript per month to review in the area. An is still working as a researcher in the field, looking at the racial/ethnic differences in the rates at which students enroll and succeed in dual enrollment efforts. However, he is frustrated that dual enrollment does not always "catch students up" to their better off peers, as the difference in the K-12 schooling they receive before their dual enrollment experience can hamper their progress. Even though dual enrollment has positive impacts for students from families with less education, equal participation of well-off and less-well-off students does little to reduce the gaps between the two groups.

Based on his research, An believes that anyone starting a dual enrollment program should take a hard look at their mission, and focus on the students and families that really need the intervention. For well-off and well-educated families, AP classes will meet their needs, and dual enrollment and early college efforts should take on the issues of lower income and less educated families. The mission of early colleges and dual enrollment programs should be to raise the odds of success for those families. He likens early college and dual enrollment programs to reflecting the ideals of community colleges – to broaden opportunities for those who need them most.

Seeking Funding for Early College Programs: State-Level Policies

How an early college is funded depends a great deal on the state in which it is located. There is a stark difference in outcomes between states that have invested early in these programs and those that have not. States such as North Carolina and Texas made large, systematic investments in early college. Beneficiaries of early Gates Foundation investment, these states expanded these programs across their cities and rural areas, creating a network of schools that had a common model, but were adapted to their circumstances. North Carolina also funds a fifth year of high school, which has also given students a leg up in college, providing up to another 30 credits (for free) before students transition to being full-time college students. The research that then has emerged from these leading states has spurred the effort of other states to catch up.

States that were part of the second wave of early college, such as Michigan, learned valuable lessons from the first wave, and built similar systems of schools, though not as extensive as the work done in Texas or North Carolina. Early college has flourished in these second-wave states as well, providing more research on the model and its impact.

The states now aiming to "catch up" on early college are those that have long considered themselves leaders in other aspects of K-12 education, such as California and Massachusetts. While these states have built many interventions, early college has been hampered by the division between K-12 and higher education systems, as well as the power of teachers' unions in both sectors. While these states have an opportunity to learn from the mistakes and problems of other systems, they need champions in the political and policy systems to build a critical mass of high-quality programs.

Potential Funding Structures

Early college and dual enrollment programs have been funded in a variety of ways, ranging from full support by state government, to mixed support between governments and philanthropy, to models where students and families bear part of the costs. There are several important options for early colleges and dual enrollment in terms of funding, listed below:

1. Tuition and scholarship model. Dual enrollment programs have typically started and grown with this approach, in which students pay extra fees to take the high school class for college credit, which offsets the costs of administering the program and training the high school staff. As concerns about equity have grown, top programs have looked to using some of the revenue to create scholarships for needy students, particularly those in urban schools or schools with a high free and reduced lunch rate. University of Connecticut is the leader in this regard, offering scholarships to students who need support to participate in the program.

2. District consortium model. In states without direct funding of early college or dual enrollment programs, school districts can form consortia and purchase college credits from local higher education institutions. Districts contribute based on their per-student allowance from the state and buy "seats" in the program each year for the early college. The consortium negotiates a discounted rate with the college and rents space at the college for program offices. As long as all participating schools and the higher education partner remain committed to the program, this model allows the flexibility for districts too small to create their own program to offer early college opportunities.
3. Public charter school model. Some programs have taken the opportunity to become their own school/district through the charter school model. This often comes with a dedicated state or local funding stream per student. While this can be a strong model for community colleges that plan a full-day program for students, it detaches the early college/dual enrollment program from local schools, and sets early college programs up as a competitor for resources.
4. Public school model. For schools in the Bard Early College Network, the preference is for the early college high school to be a regular public school, part of the school system itself. This model allows for maximum collaboration within the K-12 system, and does not set early college apart as an elite option. However, low per pupil spending can make it difficult to start or sustain a program long-term using this model.
5. Direct state funding model. States that have provided direct per pupil payments for early college programs have seen the quickest growth of these institutions and longest staying power. Having early college funding as a part of the state education budget, without having numerous workarounds and pass-through relationships, clearly indicates state support for these projects, and encourages schools and colleges to invest resources and energy in this area.
6. Fifth year of high school model. States that have allowed early college students to take a fifth year of high school have allowed

students to earn more credits at no cost to them or their family (the state fully funds this effort). Particularly in STEM fields, the extra year of support while taking college classes has meant both higher enrollment rates and a better chance of success in STEM majors.
7. Philanthropic funding. In some states, foundation funding has filled the gap for early college programs, ranging from grants to fill the gap between public school funding and what is needed to run a program, to full scale bankrolling of an early college system by a foundation. While these grants have been critical for the creation and scaling up of early college programs, they can be problematic because state and local policymakers avoid making long-term sustained commitment to early college programs.

What You Can Do When You Need Funds and Support for your Program

No matter the approach, early college programs may have gaps in their funding. How can community/business partners support early college efforts? A few ways to build support for early college initiatives include:

Start Now: In today's media and political climate, it is important to publicize "quick wins" as you go, not waiting for milestones such as a first graduation or a big evaluation report. This is difficult for those of us used to working in program evaluation, where it is customary to wait for detailed outcomes before presenting a program to the public. Instead, as good things happen, even modest in scale, it is critical to get the word out about what you are doing and get your program attention for the good it has already started to do.

Build Buzz: High-quality photos, materials, and videos can really help people connect to the effort. Parents and students often do not know about newer options, and they need to see some of the real students involved in order to believe that they can do it. Getting the college/university or district publicity staff, no matter how small, behind your effort is key to getting the word out about your effort.

Donations: Whether it is a six-figure check, or the gift of lab coats and goggles, building support from corporations, philanthropy, and other groups is critical for long-term success.

Connections to Career: When community partners can offer internships, job shadowing, job speakers, tours, it helps students connect what they are doing in math class to the real world. Government agencies such as workforce development boards can be critical here, aligning early college experiences with real workplace opportunities, such as summer employment.

Building Political Support: Schools are poorly set up to advance the cause of early colleges. Local officeholders, business people, and colleges are often good at getting the ear of lawmakers and education officials, and using it to build long-term support for funding these efforts. I invite local state representatives to talk to our early college government class every term in order to personalize the students who are benefiting from the program. This kind of firsthand testimony is key, particularly when your effort lacks the lobbying dollars that competing reform efforts have.

Grants and Gifts: Be prepared to apply to multiple funders for grants and gifts. While not all funders are open to the idea of early college, the metrics you can provide about the success of your program will help you make progress with local, state, and national foundations and funding agencies. Draw on the research evidence found throughout this book to help you make your case!

Building Support: It Starts with a Step or Two ...

Gaining funds and support for early college and dual enrollment programs can be a daunting task, particularly for beginners in areas such as evaluation and grant writing. The first step in the process is to create and run an excellent program that meets the needs of your student. From there, do not be afraid to start small in building support and, gradually, with experience, scale your efforts to match the needs of your program. Remember that hundreds of programs have been in your shoes and reach out to your colleagues for advice and support in this area.

Resource Toolbox

An, B.P. (2013). The Impact of Dual Enrollment on College Degree Attainment: Do Low-SES Students Benefit? *Educational Evaluation and Policy Analysis*, *35*(1), 57–75. doi: 10.3102/0162373712461933

Atchison, D., Zeiser, K.L., Mohammed, S., Knight, D.S. and Levin, J. (2019). The Costs and Benefits of Early College High Schools. *Education Finance and Policy*, 1–56. doi: 10.1162/edfp_a_00310

For Product Safety Concerns and Information please contact our EU representative GPSR@taylorandfrancis.com
Taylor & Francis Verlag GmbH, Kaufingerstraße 24, 80331 München, Germany

www.ingramcontent.com/pod-product-compliance
Lightning Source LLC
Chambersburg PA
CBHW051527230426
43668CB00012B/1768